460.24 21

1I8663916

Spanish Lingo

for the Savvy Gringo

A Do-It-Yourself Guide to the
Language, Culture and Slang

Elizabeth Reid, MA, DRe

Spanish Lingo for the Savvy Gringo

Sunbelt Publications, Inc.
Third Edition, Fourth printing 2005
First edition, 1991
Copyright © 1991, 1997 by Elizabeth Reid
Printed in the United States of America,

All rights reserved. No part of this book may be reproduced in any form or by any means, without permission in writing from the publisher. Es Propiedad. La propiedad de esta obra est protegida por la ley, y se perseguir a quienes la reproduzcan fraudulentamente en cualquier forma.

Please direct comments and inquiries to:

Sunbelt Publications, Inc.
P.O. Box 191126
San Diego, CA 92159-1126
(619) 258-4911, fax: (619) 258-4916
www.sunbeltbooks.com

08 07 06 05   7 6 5 4

Library of Congress Cataloging-in-Publication Data

Reid, Elizabeth, 1949-
   Spanish lingo for the savvy gringo : a do-it-yourself guide to the language, culture and slang / by Elizabeth Reid.— 3rd ed.
      v. cm.
   Third ed. of: Border Spanish. c1989.
   Contents: Courtesy — Wily vowels — The alphabet — Letter duos — The telephone — On the phone — Spanish you don't know you know — The family — The garden — Groceries — Seafood — Cooking — Painless Spanish — Weather — Winter — Christmas — Las posadas — La salud —Diet and exercise — Beyond Mr. and Mrs. — Clothing — Damaged clothing— More clothing — Housing — Housework — Home repair — Driving — Mechanic — Directions — Getting lost — Cycling — Haircut — Synonyms— Humor — Summer fun.
   ISBN 0-932653-59-6
   1. Spanish language—Conversation and phrase books—English. I. Reid, Elizabeth, 1949- Border Spanish. II. Title.
PC4121 .R45 2003
438.3'421—dc21

                              2003007571

Table of Contents

Introduction

This book will teach the reader Spanish and slang and a bit about Latin American culture, especially Mexican customs, which is almost as important if one is to get along in another country. **Spanish Lingo for the Savvy Gringo** is not like most Spanish grammar books. It is in a readable form and gives the vocabulary related to a particular topic so that you can study the words that you most need right now.

The pronunciation is given after the first time a word is used in each chapter. I have attempted to write the pronunciation without a lot of technical, dictionary symbols. The stressed syllable is in capital letters in the pronunciation. The representation of the sound may be less than perfect, but it will give you an idea of how the word should sound. There is no substitute for actually listening to the language.

The chapters do not have to be read in any special order. You can choose the subject that most interests you at the moment and plunge in. There is a variety of vocabulary, from very basic to intermediate, so that it will appeal to students of many levels. And it can be read through several times, each time reinforcing the words you already know and picking up new ones.

The Spanish in this book is that which is spoken in Mexico and frequently in the United States. This is not pure Castilian Spanish. It is however, the most widely spoken and understood in the U.S. If you are going to learn a foreign language, you might as well learn one that you will use. For people living in North America the Spanish that you get a chance to speak and understand, almost daily, is American Spanish. If you do get a chance to speak with Spaniards or South Americans, they will understand you and you will be able to understand them if you learn **Spanish Lingo for the Savvy Gringo**. There are some minor regional differences in vocabulary and accent, but they usually do not impede communication. Just as a person from Maine can understand a Texan, or a Californian can communicate with a Scotsman, the regional accents are distinctive and even charming.

As far as pronunciation, remember that "ñ" is pronounced as "ny" in "canyon," "ll" is pronounced as "y." "J" is always pronounced as "h;" "h" is always silent, an initial "g" is pronounced as "h," unless followed by "u," in which case the diphthong is pronounced almost like "w." If a word ends in "l" or "r" it is accented on the last syllable. All other words are accented on the second to last syllable unless another syllable bears an accent mark. Vowels are simple, pure, and always pronounced the same:
a—as in "ah" or "mama"
e—like the long "a" in "make" or "way"
i—like the long "e" in "feel" or "see"
o—as in "old" or "no"
u—without the initial "y" sound, as in "kudos" or "rude".

The illustrations are taken from Pre-columbian art of the Aztecs, Incas, Mayans and other indigenous peoples. Many have been sketched from stone carvings at archeological sites.

Learning a little *español (es-pahn-YOL)* (Spanish) will make a big difference in how much you enjoy your time in Mexico or anywhere in Latin America. You will make lots of friends among the people even if your efforts are less than perfect. As you learn new words, use them every chance you get so that they will become part of your permanent vocabulary. And don't forget that *por favor (por fah-VOR)* (please) and *gracias (GRAH-see-ahs)* (thank you) will work magic. Spanish-speaking people are profuse with courtesy and flowery expressions.

Learning *español* can be a real adventure and a lot of fun. It doesn't have to be a lot of work. I hope you enjoy it.
Elizabeth Reid

Chapter 1

Courtesy ...
La Cortesía

In addition to the usual **por favor** *(por fah-VOR)* (please), **gracias** *(GRAH-see-ahs)* (thank you) and **de nada** *(day NAH-dah)* (you're welcome), there are lots of useful phrases in Spanish which are used over and over again. Many of the courteous phrases cannot be translated word for word, like **de nada** which literally means "for nothing."

In English we use "excuse me" or "pardon me" in many situations, but there are different expressions in **español** which translate as "excuse me." If you accidentally step on **el pie** *(el PEE-ay)* (the foot) **de álguien** *(day ALL-ghee-en)* (of someone), you say, **"dispénseme usted"** *(dees-PEN-say-may oo-STED)* (excuse me) or **"perdóneme"** *(pair-DOH-nay-may)* (pardon me).

Now, **supongamos** *(soo-pon-GAH-mos)* (let's suppose) that you want to avoid stepping on **el pie de álguien** but you need to get past some people. You **don't** say **dispénseme** or **perdóneme.** You say, **"Con su permiso"** *(kohn soo* *pair-MEE-so)* (excuse me, or literally "with your permission").

If somebody speaks to you but you don't hear them and you want them to repeat what they said, you say *"¿Mande usted?" (MAIIN-day oo STED)* (excuse me, or literally "at your command") or *"¿Digame?" (DEE-guh-may)* (literally, tell me). So there are different expressions to say "pardon me" or "excuse me" in three different situations in Spanish. If *álguien* calls your name you can also respond with *"Mande usted"* or just *"Mande."* If they are calling you to come, you can say, *"Allí voy" (i-YEE voy)* (*I'm coming, or here I come, although Spanish uses the verb ir,* "to go").

When you are talking to *fulano (foo-LA-no)* (what's-his-name) and you are getting ready to leave, you say, *"Ya me voy" (yah may voy)* (I'm leaving already). In Mexico *la gente (la HEN-tay)* (the people) frequently say *"ya me voy"* two or three times before they actually leave. Be patient! It doesn't mean that they are actually walking out the door, it means that they are getting ready to leave.

In ending a conversation, when *fulano* says, *"Gusto en saludarte" (GOO-sto en sah-loo-DAR-tay)* (It's been a pleasure to see you or greet you), you might respond, *"Nos vemos" (nos VAY-mos)* (I'll be seeing you—in Spanish "we'll see each other"). Many people will add *"Primero Dios" (pree-MAY-ro dee-OHS)* (God willing) or *"Dios mediante" (dee-OHS may-dee-AHN-tay)* (with God's help).

In some situations *primero Dios* can also be translated as "I hope so" instead of *espero (es-PAY-ro)* (I hope, from the verb *esperar*). For example, *"Primero Dios que no llueve" (pree-MAY-ro dee-OHS kay no yoo-WAY-vay)* (I hope it doesn't rain or, may it please God that it doesn't rain). Some people prefer this to *ojalá (oh-ha-LA)* which is roughly interchangeable with *primero Dios. Ojalá* means "may Allah grant it" and entered the language during the Moorish invasion of the Iberian peninsula. Which expression you use depends upon whether you are particular about which god you invoke, the Judeo-Christian or the Moslem, although most people have forgotten that *ojalá* refers to Allah.

Use these expressions liberally in your Spanish conversations and everyone will think you are very *bien educado (bee-EN ay-doo-KAH-doh)* (well bred). Latin culture is extremely *cortés (kor-TAYS)* (courteous) and it is almost impossible to overdo it.

Chapter 2

Wily Vowels: Vocales Tramposos

When learning Spanish, it is important to pay close attention to the pronunciation of a new word. Slight changes in the vowels can make an entirely different word and meaning—with sometimes hilarious results. For example, *hombre (OHM-bray)* (man), *hambre (AHM-bray)* (hunger) and *hombro (OHM-bro)* (shoulder) all sound similar. But don't tell the waitress, *"Tengo hombre,"* (literally "I have man"); tell her, *"Tengo hambre"* (literally, "I have hunger"—this is the correct way to say that you are hungry).

The English-speaker's ear is not accustomed to listening for vowels at the end of words because there are so few in our language. But the final *vocal (vo-KALL)* (vowel) in Spanish can make a big difference. It differentiates sexes, as students quickly learn: *muchacho (moo-CHA-cho)* (boy), *muchacha (moo-CHA-cha)* (girl). More sex-change operations take place due to careless Spanish pronunciation than Swedish doctors ever imagined!

Sometimes a different final vowel changes the meaning, too. When getting directions, listen carefully. Then don't go *derecha (day-RAY-cha)* (right) if they said to go *derecho (day-RAY-cho)* (straight ahead). Never invite anyone to a *banqueta (bahn-KAY-tah)* (sidewalk) when you really want to say *banquete (bahn-KAY-tay)* (banquet). And don't wear *botes (BO-tays)* (tin cans) if you mean to wear *botas (BO-tahs)* (boots) to the rodeo. Don't change *el llanto (el YAHN-toh)* (the crying) if *la llanta (la YAHN-tah)* (the tire) is flat. And don't open *el puerto (el PWAYR-toh)* (the port or harbor) if someone knocks on *la puerta (la PWAYR-tah)* (the door).

When dealing with *policía (po-lee-SEE-ah)* (police), *el policía* indicates a specific officer while *la policía* refers to the whole department. *La policía investiga el caso (een-ves-TEE-gah el KAH-so)* (the police investigate the case). *El policía viene a la casa (vee-EH-nay ah la KAH-sah)* (the policeman comes to the house). Here are more words that are similar: *caso* (case) and *casa* (house), not to mention *cosa (KO-sah)* (thing).

Many words just sound similar: *cereza (say-RAY-sah)* (cherry) and *cerveza (sair-VAY-sah)* (beer); *cuarto (KWAR-toh)* (room), *cuadra (KWAH-drah)* (block), *cuadro (KWAH-dro)* (picture) and *cuatro (KWAH-troh)* (four); *saludo (sah-LOO-doh)* (greeting), *salado (sah-LA-doh)* (salty) and *salúd (sah-LOOD)* (health—it's what you say if someone sneezes); *viaje (vee-AH-hay)* (trip), *viejo (vee-AY-ho)* (old) and *vigésimo (vee-HAY-see-mo)* (twentieth). By the way, *anciano (ahn-see-AH-no)* is a more polite way to refer to an older person than *viejo*. Yet *viejo* is used in the sense of referring to one's spouse as the old man (*viejo*) or the old lady (*vieja*) regardless of their actual age, and far from giving offense, is a term of endearment. Confused yet? Imagine how your Spanish-speaking aquaintances feel when you ask room service to send "a cherry to your four for your trip" instead of "a beer to your room for your spouse."

There are still more words that sound similar: *lentes (LEN-tays)* (eye glasses), *lento (LEN-toh)* (slow), *lenteja (len-TAY-ha)* (lentil) and *lentejuela (len-tay-HWAY-lay)* (sequin); *cansado (kahn-SAH-doh)* (tired), *candado (kahn-DAH-doh)* (padlock), *casado (kah-SAH-doh)* (married), *condado (kohn-DAH-doh)* (county) and *cadena (kah-DAY-nah)* (chain). *Dos (dohs)* (two) sounds a lot like *tos (tohs)* (cough); *espada (es-PA-dah)* (sword) like *espalda (es-PALL-dah)* (back); *amar (ah-MAR)* (to love) like *amarrar (ah-mar-RAR)* (to tie). *Cabello (kah-BAY-yo)* (hair) is like *caballo (kah-BY-yo)* (horse) and even a little like *cebolla (say-BOY-yah)* (onion). *Comezón (ko-may-SOHN)* (itching) and *camisón (kah-mee-SOHN)* (nightgown) are like *comienzo (ko-mee-EN-so)* (I begin, from *comenzar*) and *comiendo (ko-mee-EN-doh)* (eating, from the verb *comer*).

Sometimes an accent mark is the only difference between two words with very different meanings. When the word is only one syllable, you can't even hear the accent: *él* (he) and *el* (the); *sí* (yes) and *si* (if). With two or more syllables you can hear the difference: *esta (ES-tah)* (this) and *está (es-TAH)* (is, from *estar*); *hacia (AH-see-ah)* (toward) and *hacía (ah-SEE-ah)* (made, from *hacer*). And that silent "h" adds to the difficulty: *Asia (AH-see-ah)* (Asia) sounds just like *hacia*.

So pay close attention to what you hear and how you pronounce in Spanish. Of course, the context will help. There's a world of difference between *una maleta (OO-nah ma-LAY-tah)* (a suitcase) and *una muleta (OO-nah moo-LAY-tah)* (a crutch)! You don't always want to leave them laughing.

Chapter 3

The Alphabet: El Alfabeto

Learning **el alfabeto** *(el all-fah-BAY-toh)* (the alphabet) in **español** may seem superfluous, but it can come in handy. Knowing **el abecedario** *(el ah-bay-say-DAH-ree-oh)* (the abc's) is useful in learning new words and when someone wants you to **deletrear** *(day-lay-tray-AR)* (to spell) your **apellido** *(ah-pay-YEE-doh)* (last name). After all, you don't want to look like **un analfabeto** *(oon ah-nall-fah-BAY-toh)* (an illiterate). So here's a list of the Spanish **abecedario** and its pronunciation:

a	ah
b	bay
c	say
ch	chay (no longer a letter, but here for pronunciation)
d	day
e	ay
f	EH-fay
g	hay

h	AH- chay
i	ee
j	HO-tah
k	kah
l	EH-lay
ll	AY-yay (no longer a letter, but here for pronunciation)
m	EH-may
n	EH-nay
ñ	EN-yay
o	oh
p	pay
q	k oo
r	EH-ray
rr	AIR-ray
s	EH-say
t	tay
u	oo
v	vay
w	doh-blay-OO
x	EH-kees
y	ee-gree-AY-gah
z	SEH-tah

Se da cuenta (say dah KWEN-tah) (you notice) that there are 30 *letras (LAY-trahs)* (letters) instead of 26. As in *inglés*, some *letras* sound very similar. For example, when somebody is *deletreando (day-lay-tray-AHN-doh)* (spelling) *barro (BAR-ro)* (mud, clay), you might hear, *"b grande" (bay GRAHN-day)* (literally big "b")—this does not mean *"b mayúscula" (bay my-OO-skoo-la)* (capital "b") as you might think. It is to differentiate between *"b" grande* and *"v" chica (bay CHEE-kah)* (literally small "v"). The "b" and "v" are pronounced so much alike that they both come out "bay" frequently. In English we say, "b as in boy" and "v as in Victor." Another way to say this is *"b" de burro (bay day BOOR-ro)* ("b" as in "burro") or *"v" de vaca (vay day VAH-kah)* ("v" as in "cow"). The *"b" de burro* is taken as a joke between friends, but be careful—it could be interpreted as an insult: that you are saying that the person is *muy burro (MOO-ee BOOR-ro)* (very stupid).

There seems to be a lot of confusion among "c," "k," and "q," so expressions have been devised to distinguish among these *letras*. **Se oye** *(say OH-yay)* (you hear) of **"c" de casa** *(say day KAH-sah)* ("c" as in house), **"k" de kilo** *(kah day KEE-lo)* ("k" as in kilo) and **"q" de queso** *(koo day KAY-so)* ("q" as in cheese). Using expressions like these when spelling in Spanish will make you look like a real linguist. People will say that you are **un estuche de monerías** *(oon es-TOO-chay day mo-nay-REE-ahs)* (a bag of tricks or literally, a case of monkeyshines). Or they may say that you are **una caja de sorpresas** *(OO-nah KAH-ha day sor-PRAY-sahs)* (a box of surprises).

A propósito *(ah pro-PO-see-toh)* (by the way), "k" and "w" were not originally in the Spanish *alfabeto*. They appear primarily in words **prestado** *(pray-STAH-doh)* (borrowed) from other languages. That's why those sections of **el diccionario** are so **breve** *(BRAY-vay)* (short or brief).

When distinguishing between "rr" and "r" it is perfectly all right to say **doble "r"** *(DOH-blay EH-ray)* (double "r") or **una sola "r"** *(OO-nah SO-la EH-ray)* (just one "r"). But this is unnecessary with "l" and "ll" as they sound so different when you say them. Occasionally you might confuse "i" and "y." This is fairly easy. The "y" is known as **"y" griega** *(ee-gree-AY-gah)* (Greek "i") and the regular "i" is called **"i" latina** *(ee la-TEE-nah)* (Latin "i").

While **la ortografía** *(la or-toh-grah-FEE-ah)* (spelling) in Spanish is quite simple when compared to English with all its silent letters and exceptions to rules, it is still a bit of a challenge. Remember that place names and proper names are written with **mayúscula** but in **español**, days of the week, months and nationalities are written with **minúscula** *(mee-NOO-skoo-la)* (lower case) letters.

Of course, speaking and understanding Spanish is primary. Practice **el abecedario** until you know the letters out of order. Then try **deletreando** your name in Spanish. It's trickier than you might think!

Chapter 4

Letter Duos:
Letras Dobles

While English words frequently have double consonants for no obvious reason, Spanish words do not, with *la excepción (ek-sep-see-OHN)* (the exception) of "ll" and "rr" (which have been considered single letters) and "cc" as in *acción (ahk-see-OHN)* (action). (In 1994 the Association of Spanish Language Academies decided that "ll" and "ch" are no longer separate letters.)

The three letter combinations which Spanish considered single letters until 1994 (the other one is "ch") can cause confusion when looking up something in an alphabetical list, as in *el directorio (el dee-rek-TOH-ree-oh)* (the phone directory) or *el diccionario (el deek-see-oh-NAH-ree-oh)* (the dictionary). *Llamar (yah-MAR)* (to call) came after *luna (LOO-nah)* (the moon) because "ll" was the letter after "l" and before "m." Since changes like this take time, an nobody in Latin America is in a hurry, you will likely find many instances where the "ll" and "ch" are still treated as letters; no words begin with "rr" but words beginning with "r" have a stronger "r" sound.

It is important to pronounce "ll" as a "y" sounds in English, especially when learning *español* from written material. The English-speaking brain automatically pronounces "l" no matter how many "l's" there are. Failure to distinguish can mean a different word entirely. For example, *el loro (el LO-ro)* (the parrot) and *lloro (YO-ro)* (I cry, from the verb *llorar)*; *la lana (la LA-nah)* (wool, or slang for cash) and *el llano (el YAH-no)* (a flat or level surface, a plain); *lavar (la-VAR)* (to wash), *llevar (yay-VAR)* (to carry) and *la llave (la YAH-vay)* (the key); *llegar (yay-GAR)* (to arrive) and *lograr (lo-GRAR)* (to attain).

When the "ll" is in the middle of the word it is even more important to give it the proper emphasis: *la calle (la KY-yay)* (the street) and *callar (ky-YAR)* (to shut up, to be quiet) are different from *caer (kah-AIR)* (to fall); *la olla (la OY-yah)* (the pot), *la ola (la OH-la)* (the wave), *el hoyo (el OY-oh—remember, the "h" is silent)* (the pit) and *la jolla (la HOY-yah)* (the jewel—sometime spelled *joya)*; *el muelle (el MWAY-yay)* (the pier or dock) and *la muela (la MWAY-la)* (the molar or tooth); *la villa (la VEE-yah)* (the villa), *la vía (la vee-ah)* (the way or track), *el valle (el VAH-yay)* (the valley).

To pronounce the "ll" in the middle of the word and distinguish it from a similar word, you must say a strong "y." Some accents verge on a "j" sound. *Ahí (ah-EE)* and *allí (ah-YEE)* mean the same thing (there), but other words are not so accommodating: *vía* and *villa*, *hoyo* and *olla*, *ansia (AHN-see-ah)* (longing) and *ensillar (en-see-YAR)* (to saddle).

This special sound which English-speakers' ears resist hearing is a part of the suffix *illo* or *illa* which means something small or dear, as do the suffixes *ito* and *ita*. The *illo* suffix is part of some words long-forgotten to have been modified with the ending: *la cerilla (la say-REE-yah)* (the match) is literally a small candle, because many matches in

Mexico and Spain are made of *cera (SAY-rah)* (wax). Be careful not to roll the "r" too much. A favorite way of depicting the *gringo* accent in cartoons is having the "rr" sound when only the "r" is called for.

Which brings us to the bane of all English-speaking mouths that are trying to wrap themselves around Spanish: "rr." This is the only sound in Spanish that we do not have in English. In *español* the "r" is sounded in the mouth instead of the throat—almost like "d" or the "t" sound in "butter." The "rr" is the same, only more of it: a trilling of the tongue. It is worth practicing, however, because, like "l" and "ll," it can mean a completely different word. Try listening for the difference in pronunciation when you hear native speakers use these words: *el cerro (el SAIR-roh)* (the hill), *la cera* and *cerrar (sair-RAR)* (to close); *pero (PEH-ro)* (but) and *el perro (el PAIR-ro)* (dog); *oro (OH-ro)* (gold), *ahora (ah-OH-rah)* (now), and *ahorrar (ah-ohr-RAR)* (to save); *caro (KAH-ro)* (expensive) and *el carro (el KAR-ro)* (the car).

By paying close attention to the Spanish you hear, you can improve your own use of *el idioma (el ee-dee-OH-ma)* (the language). And you'll fine-tune your "r's" and "rr's." You don't want to *enterrar (en-tair-RAR)* (to bury) when you mean to *enterar (en-tay-RAR)* (to inform). Communication is what it's all about.

Chapter 5

The Telephone
... *El Teléfono*

Talking *en el teléfono (en el tay-LAY-fo-no)* (on the telephone) is sometimes necessary and a little scary if you don't speak much *español*. Here are some phrases to help you. Don't get *desilusionado (day-see-loo-see-oh-NAH-doh)* (disappointed) if it is not easy. *Hablar por teléfono (ah-BLAR por tay-LAY-fo-no)* (speaking by phone) is difficult to master in another language. There are no visual cues: no *caras (KAH-rahs)* (faces), no *bocas (BO-kahs)* (mouths), no *ademanes (ah-day-MA-nays)* (gestures); only what you hear. So you'll need to *practicar (prahk-tee-KAR)* (practice) these phrases *mucho (MOO-cho)* (a lot).

To *contestar (kohn-tays-TAR)* (answer) *el teléfono* you say, *"Bueno" (BWAY-no)* (literally "good") in Mexico, not *"Hola" (OH-la)* (hello). Most businesses also say the name of the company. Some residences will say the name of

la familia (la fah-MEE-lee-ah) (the family). For example,
"Bueno, familia Romo Moreno." You may also hear
"Diga" (DEE-gah) (speak or tell) when you make a call.
It is common to hear, *"¿Quién habla?" (kee-EN
AH blah)* (who is speaking?). When someone asks this you
may reply, *"Habla ____" (AH-blah___) (___* is speaking). Put your name in the blank. Or, you can just say your
name. It is polite to say, *Buenos días, Buenas tardes,* or
Buenas noches, and to ask about the answering party's
health: *"¿Cómo está usted?"* This all precedes the motive
for the call.

To ask for someone you say, *"¿Está ____?" (es-
TAH____) (Is _____* there?). Or, you can say, *"Quiero
hablar con ____" (kee-AY-ro ah-BLAR kohn ___)* (I want
to speak to____). If that person is there you will usually
hear, *"Sí, un momento" (see oon mo-MEN-toh)* (yes, one
moment). Then, with a little luck, you'll hear *la voz (la
vohs)* (the voice) of your *amigo.* Alternatively, if that person
answered the *teléfono,* he will say, *"él habla" (el AH-blah)*
(he is speaking), or *ella habla (AY-yah AH-blah)* (she is
speaking). Okay, so far we have a conversation that goes
like this:

» Jorge: *Bueno. Familia González.*
Gloria: *Buenos días. ¿Quién habla?*
Jorge: *Habla Jorge González.*
Gloria: *Hola. Habla Gloria. ¿Como está usted,
Jorge?*
Jorge: *Bien, ¿y usted?*
Gloria: *Bien, gracias. ¿Está Elena?*
Jorge: *Sí, un momento.*

Practice this several times with a friend. Take turns
being the one to *contestar (kohn-tes-TAR)* (answer) or the
one to *hablar.*

Now suppose you say, *"Quiero hablar con Elena"*
and the reply is, *"No está" (no es-TAH)* (she or he is not
here). You may want to let her know that you called.
"Quiero dejar un mensaje" (kee-AY-ro day-HAR oon men-

SAH-hay) (I want to leave a message). *Favor de decirle que llamé (fah-VOR day day-SEER-lay kay yah-MAY)* (please tell her or him that I called).

When you have to *marcar (mar-KAR)* (to dial) *el número (el NOO-may-ro)* (the number), do it carefully. If you don't, you'll hear, *"Usted marcó mal" (oo-STED mar-KO mall)* (you dialed wrong, or wrong number). *No cuelgue (no KWAYL-gay)* (don't hang up, from the verb *colgar*) until you say , *"Disculpe" (dees-KOOL-pay)* (pardon me).

By the way, when you say *un número de teléfono* in Spanish it's not digit by digit as in *inglés*. The numbers are said two by two, much the way we say an address in English. For example, *ochenta y cuarto—cero tres—veintidós (oh-CHEN-tah ee KWAH-tro SAY-ro trays bayn-tee-DOHS)* (84-03-22). *Números* in large cities in Mexico have six digits, in smaller towns they have only five digits. A small town number might be *ocho—treinta y cinco—sesenta y nueve (OH-cho TRAYN-tah ee SEEN-ko say-SEN-tah ee noo-WAY-vay)* (8-35-69). To correctly give and take down *números de teléfono* you'll need the numbers in Spanish from *cero (SAY-ro)* (zero) to *noventa y nueve (no-VAYN-tah ee noo-WAY-vay)* (ninety-nine). Here's a list to study:

0	*cero* (SAY-roh)
1	*uno (OO-no)*
2	*dos (dohs)*
3	*tres (trays)*
4	*cuatro (KWAH-tro)*
5	*cinco (SEEN-ko)*
6	**seis** *(says)*
7	*siete (see-EH-tay)*
8	*ocho (OH-cho)*
9	*nueve (n oo-WAY-vay)*
10	*diez (dee-AYS)*
11	*once (OHN-say)*
12	*doce (DOH-say)*
13	*trece (TRAY-say)*
14	*catorce (kah-TOR-say)*
15	*quince (KEEN-say)*

16   *diez y seis (dee-ES ee SAYS)*
17   *diez y siete (dee-ES ee see-EH-tay)*
18   *diez y ocho (dee-ES ee OH-cho)*
19   *diez y nueve (dee-ES ee noo-WAY-vay)*
20   *veinte (BAYN-tay)*
21   *veintiuno (bayn-tee-UU-no)*
22   *veintidós (bayn-tee-DOHS)*
23   *veintitrés (bayn-tee-TRAYS)*
24   *veinticuatro (bayn-tee-KWAH-tro)*
25   *veinticinco (bayn-tee-SEEN-ko)*
26   *veintiséis (bayn-tee-SAYS)*
27   *veintisiete (bayn-tee-see-EH-tay)*
28   *veintiocho (bayn-tee-OH-cho)*
29   *veintinueve (bayn-tee-noo-WAY-vay)*
30   *treinta (TRAYN-tah)*
31   *treinta y uno (TRAYN-tah ee OO-no)*
32   *treinta y dos (TRAYN-tah ee dohs)*
33   *treinta y tres (TRAYN-tah ee TRAYS)*
34   *treinta y cuatro (TRAYN-tah ee KWAH-tro)*
40   *cuarenta (kwah-REN-tah)*
50   *cincuenta (seen-KWEN-tah)*
60   *sesenta (say-SEN-tah)*
70   *setenta (say-TEN-tah)*
80   *ochenta (oh-CHEN-tah)*
90   *noventa (no-VEN-tah)*

You should become familiar enough with these *números* that you know them even when they are out of order. Learning to count is one thing—and an important one. But learning numbers is another. It may help you to practice counting backward. Then you will be ready when you see a *señorita bonita (sen-yo-REE-tah bo-NEE-tah)* (pretty single woman), you can ask her, *"¿Qúe es su número de teléfono?"* (what's your phone number). And you'll be ready to understand her answer.

Chapter 6

On the Phone:
En el Teléfono

After studying the previous chapter, you should be able to understand these simple phone conversations. Practice them with a friend a few times to improve your speaking ability. It takes a lot of practice to speak with fluency, and it takes even more practice to be able to understand Spanish on *el teléfono* when you can't see the person with whom you are speaking.

In order to **mejorar** *(may-ho-RAR)* (improve) your comprehension, don't agree in advance which conversation you will do. Then it will be a surprise whether the person is at home for the **llamada** *(yah-MA-dah)* (call).

> *(tin . . .tin . . .tin)*
> *Alfonso: ¡Bueno!*
> *René: Buenos días. ¿Se encuentra el Sr. Torres?*
> *Alfonso: Sí. ¿Quién habla?*

René: Habla René Gomez.
Alfonso: Un momento, por favor.

(tin . . .tin . . .tin)
Jonás· ¡Bueno!
Griselda: Buenas tardes. ¿Se encuentra Mónica?
Jonás: No, no se encuentra ahorita. No está en
casa.
Griselda: Favor de decirle que llamó Griselda.
Jonás: ¿Ella tiene su número de teléfono?
Griselda: No. Mi número es el 85-32-64. Gracias.
Jonás: Por nada. Adiós.

There are only a couple of new words here. **Recado**
(ray-KAH-doh) (message) is the same as **mensaje**. **Se encuentra** *(say en-KWEN-trah)* (literally, do you find) is another way of saying **está** when you ask if someone is home.
And **decir** *(day-SEER)* (to tell) takes the indirect object **le**
(her or him) and tacks it on to the end of the infinitive,
making one word, **decirle** (tell her or tell him).

Now when you make a **llamada** and your **amigo no
está**, you can leave **un recado**. Speaking on the telephone is
difficult! **No cuelgue.**

Chapter 7

Spanish You Don't Know You Know

I have **un amigo** *(oon ah-MEE-go)* (a friend) who makes us **reír** *(ray-EER)* (laugh) **a carcajadas** *(ah kar-kah-HA-dahs)* (uproariously) at *fiestas* by speaking false Spanish. He just adds an "o" to the end of every other word in English. I don't know why "I want-o **un** glass-o of water-o" is so funny. Perhaps it is because we all know how much work it is to learn **un lenguaje** *(oon len-GWAH-hay)* (a language) and this guy seems to have found the perfect short cut. His rhythm and intonation are flawless, but the words aren't Spanish.

However, there are a lot of words that are **igual** *(ee-GWALL)* (equal, the same) or **muy similar** *(MOO-ee*

see-mee-LAR) (very similar) between the two languages.
These are called cognates and when you see one *escrito
(es-KREE-toh)* (written), you know right away the meaning
of the word, *aunque (OWN-kay)* (although) the pronunciation may be very *diferente (dee-fay-REN-tay)* (different).
You can boost your *vocabulario (vo-kah-boo-LA-ree-oh)*
(vocabulary) by learning the Spanish pronunciation. Then
practice listening for cognates when you hear *el español*
spoken.

Here's a list with the way to say the word in Spanish.
The translation is not given because the word means just
what it looks like it means:

actor	*(ahk-TOR)*	*honor*	*(oh-NOR)*
animal	*(ah-nee-MALL)*	*horrible*	*(oh-REE-blay)*
área	*(AH-ray-ah)*	*hospital*	*(ohs-pee-TALL)*
atlas	*(AHT-las)*	*hotel*	*(oh-TAIL)*
auto	*(OW-toh)*	*humor*	*(oo-MOR)*
capital	*(kah-pee-TALL)*	*idea*	*(ee-DAY-ah)*
central	*(sen-TRALL)*	*local*	*(lo-KALL)*
cereal	*(say-ray-ALL)*	*material*	*(ma-tay-ree-ALL)*
chocolate	*(cho-ko-LA-tay)*	*melón*	*(may-L OHN)*
civil	*(see-VEEL)*	*metal*	*(may-TALL)*
color	*(ko-LOR)*	*motor*	*(mo-TOR)*
conclusión	(kohn-kloo-see-	*musical*	*(moo-see-KALL)*
OHN)		*natural*	*(nah-too-RALL)*
conductor	*(kohn-dook-TOR)*	*original*	*(oh-ree-he e-NAHL)*
cónsul	*(KOHN-sool)*	*personal*	*(pair-so-NAHL)*
cruel	*(kroo-EL)*	*plan*	*(plahn)*
director	*(dee-rayk-TOR)*	*popular*	*(po-poo-LAR)*
doctor	*(dohk-TOR)*	*principal*	*(preen-see-PAHL)*
error	*(air-ROR)*	*probable*	*(pro-BAH-blay)*
exterior	*(eks-tay-ree-OR)*	*regular*	*(ray-goo-LAR)*
familiar	*(fah-mee-lee-AR)*	*religión*	*(ray-lee-hee-OHN)*
favor	*(fah-VOR)*	*simple*	*(SEEM-play)*
final	*(fee-NALL)*	*taxi*	*(TAHK-see)*
formal	*(for-MALL)*	*terrible*	*(tair-REE-blay)*
gas	*(gahs)* (not gasoline)	*total*	*(toh-TALL)*
general	*(hen-nay-RAHL)*	*usual*	*(oos-WALL)*

Incorporating cognates into your *conversación
(kohn-vair-sah-see-OHN)* (conversation) is a practically

painless way to greatly increase your Spanish. It sounds too good to be true, doesn't it? Well, be careful! There are also false cognates that appear to be the same but are not. Here are a few to watch out for:

actual (ahk-TWALL) (present time, **not** actual)
asistir (ah-see-STEER) (to attend, **not** to assist)
colegio (ko-LAY-hee-oh) (a private elementary or high school, **not** a college)
competencia (kohm-pay-TEN-see-ah) (a competition, **not** competence)
criatura (kree-ah-TOO-rah) (a child **or** a creature)
desgracia (des-GRAH-see-ah) (misfortune, **not** disgrace)
educación (ay-doo-kah-see-OHN) (upbringing, **not** education)
embarazada (em-bah-rah-SAH-dah) (pregnant, **not** embarrassed)
estrechar (es-tray-CHAR) (to squeeze or tighten, **not** to stretch)
éxito (EK-see-toh) (success or a hit, **not** an exit)
fútbol (FOOT-bowl) (soccer, **not** football)

Make sure you know the meaning of a word before you start to use it. Even though the meaning appears to be the same as in English, it may be very different. You don't want to say that you are *embarazada* (pregnant) when you are really *avergonzado (ah-vair-gohn-SAH-doh)* (embarrassed).

Chapter 8

The Family...
La Familia

No man is an island, claimed John Donne. And no woman, either. Everyone has *parientes (pa-ree-EN-tays)* (relatives), those from whom we are descended and those who descend from us. In Latin America, the extended *familia (fa-MEE-lee-ah)* (family) is still common so if someone offers to introduce you to their *familia,* be prepared to sort out who is who. This chapter will help.

The nuclear family is, of course, *el padre (el PA-dray)* (the father), *la madre (la MA-dray)* (the mother) and *los hijos (los EE-hos)* (the sons, or sons and daughters—*las hijas* if they are all daughters). From the point of view of *el padre,* he may have *la esposa (la es-PO-sah)* (the wife) and *hijos.* He might say, *"Tengo tres hijos" (TEN-go trays EE-hos)* (I have three children); then to clarify, *"Dos hombres y una mujer" (dohs OHM-brays ee OO-na moo-HAIR).* This let's you know that he has two sons and one daughter.

It is common to refer to children as *hombre* (literally, man) and *mujer* (woman) to describe their sex. So, when *la esposa* has *un bebé (oon bay-BAY)* (a baby), it is correct to ask, *"¿Hombre o mujer?" El esposo (el es-PO-so)* or *el marido (el ma-REE-doh)* (the husband) will be proud, either way. And *los hijos* will have a new *hermano (air-MA-no)* (brother). With great efficiency the Spanish language cleverly cuts in half the number of words for relatives, making it easier to learn them all. The last letter indicates if the *pariente* is male or female—it ends in "o" if masculine and in "a" if feminine. So if *los hijos* have a new sister, she is *la hermana (la air-MA-nah)*.

El hermano del padre is *el tío (el TEE-oh)* (the uncle). If *el tío* has *hijos,* they are *los primos (los PREE-mos)* (the cousins). *La hermana del padre* is *la tía (la TEE-ah)* (the aunt). The same terms are used for *parientes* on the side of *la madre. El marido de la hermana* is *el cuñado (koon-YAH-doh)* (brother-in-law); and *la esposa del hermano* is *la cuñada (la koon-YAH-dah)* (sister-in-law).

What about the other in-laws? *La madre del esposo o la esposa* is *la suegra (la SWAY-grah)* (the mother-in-law). *El padre del marido o de la esposa* is *el suegro (el SWAY-grow)* (the father-in-law). *Los padres (los PA-drays)* (the parents) *de los padres* are *los abuelos (los ah-BWAY-los)* (the grandparents). *La abuela (la ah-BWAY-la)* (the grandmother) may spoil *los nietos (los nee-AY-tos)* (the grandchildren) with little gifts. But it is because she loves them. On the other hand, *la tía* is not usually accused of spoiling *los sobrinos (los so-BREE-nos)* (the nephews, or nephews and nieces) or *las sobrinas (las so-BREE-nahs)* (the nieces). Some Mexican *familias* are extended to the point that there are *parientes* so distant that no one is sure of the actual blood line. When introduced they may be described as *primos.*

Some couples have *divorciado (dee-vor-see-AH-doh)* (divorced) and remarried. In this way, a *madrastra (ma-DRAH-strah)* (step-mother) may bring with her *hijastros (ee-HA-stros)* (step-children) for her new *esposo.* It may not be courteous to inquire too closely as to the exact

relation of each *pariente.* If you have the honor to be introduced say, *"Mucho gusto" (MOO-cho GOO-sto)* (pleased
to meet you), and let it go at that. They are *familia* and that
is enough.

Chapter 9

The Garden: El Jardín

In *la primavera (la pree-ma-VAY-rah)* (spring), many people begin to think of *un jardín (oon har-DEEN)* (a garden). Whether you enjoy *la satisfacción (la sah-tees-fahk-see-OHN)* (the satisfaction) of serving home grown *verduras (vair-DOO-rahs)* (vegetables or greens) or just want to grow some special *vegetales (vay-hay-TAH-lays)* (vegetables) that are not readily available locally, *un jardín* can be a rewarding *pasatiempo (pa-sah-tee-EM-po)* (hobby or pastime).

Choose *un lugar soleado (oon loo-GAR so-lay-AH-doh)* (a sunny place) to put your *huerto (WAIR-toh)* (vegetable garden or orchard). Loosen *la tierra (la tee-AY-rah)* (the earth) so that it will be ready to *plantar (plahn-TAR)* (to plant). Then get *las semillas (las say-MEE-yahs)* (the seeds). What you plant will be dictated by *su gusto (soo GOO-sto)* (your taste). *Calabaza (kah-la-BAH-sah)* (all kinds of squash, including pumpkin) is an easy *hortaliza (or-tah-LEE-sah)* (vegetable plant) to grow and comes in many **variedades** *(vah-ree-ay-DAH-days)* (varieties). **Calabacitas italianas** *(kah-la-bah-SEE-tahs ee-tah-lee-AH-nahs)* (Italian squash, zucchini) are prolific, so you will have lots to **compartir** *(kohm-par-TEER)* (share) with your friends.

Perhaps you are longing for some **berenjena** *(bay-ren-HAY-nah)* (eggplant) to cook. Or, **se le antoja** *(say lay ahn-TOH-ha)* (you long for) **alcachofa** *(all-kah-CHO-fah)* (artichoke). These are sometimes hard to find. **Elote** *(ay-LO-tay)* (corn on the cob) is readily available in Latin America, but only in your own **milpa** *(MEEL-pa)* (field) are you moved to sing tunes from the show "Oklahoma!" When you are **cavando** *(kah-VAHN-doh)* (digging) with your **azadón** *(ah-sah-DOHN)* (hoe) and **sudando** *(soo-DAHN-doh)* (sweating) in your **jardín, ¡no se desanime!** *(no say day-sah-NEE-may)* (don't lose heart). Think of the fresh **chícharos** CHEE-cha-ros) (peas), **espinacas** *(es-pee-NAH-kahs)* (spinach) and **fresas** *(FRAY-sahs)* (strawberries) you are going to **cosechar** *(ko-say-CHAR)* (harvest).

And if you want **una cosecha** *(OO-nah ko-SAY-cha)* (a harvest) of **vegetales** and **frutas** *(FROO-tahs)* (fruits) that are **maduras** *(ma-DOO-rahs)* (ripe) and **grandes** *(GRAHN-days)* (big), don't forget to **regar** *(ray-GAR)* (water, irrigate) and **abonar** *(ah-bo-NAR)* (fertilize—the same word refers to paying in installments. **Comprar en abonos**, to buy on the installment plan, compares with **pagar al contado**, to pay the full amount).

A true gourmet, you will want to use fresh **hierbas** *(YAIR-bahs)* (herbs) from **el jardín** when cooking. **Cebollino** *(say-boy-YEE-no)* (chives), **orégano** *(oh-RAY-gah-no)* (you guessed it: oregano), **sálvia** *(SAL-vee-ah)* (sage), **perejil** *(pay-ray-HEEL)* (parsley), and **ajo** *(AH-hoh)* (garlic) will add flavor to **ensaladas** *(en-sah-LA-dahs)* (salads) and other **manjares** *(mahn-HA-rays)* (dishes). **Yerba buena** *(YAIR-bah BWAY-nah)* (mint) is a hardy herb and, like **cilantro** *(see-LAHN-tro)* (fresh coriander), is best when just picked. Even **girasol** *(hee-rah-SOL)* (sunflower) can find a place in your **huerto**.

If **cultivar** *(kool-tee-VAR)* (growing) your own **verduras** isn't for you, these words will still help you when buying **en el supermercado** *(en el soo-pair-mair-KAH-doh)* (in the supermarket) or when ordering **en un restaurante** *(en oon rest-ow-RAHN-tay)* (in a restaurant). Pronounce with care: In Mexico **ejote** *(ay-HO-tay)* is green beans, similar to **elote** (fresh corn). Either way you get a **vegetal**, but it may not be what you had in mind.

Chapter 10

Groceries: Abarrotes

Shopping in Mexico and Latin America can be a lot of fun, and not just in *las tiendas de curiosidades (las tee-EN-dahs day KOO-ree-oh-see-dah-days)* (the curio shops). Even *el supermercado (el soo-pair-mair-KAH-doh)* (the supermarket) can be an adventure. *Tarde o temprano (TAR-day oh tem-PRAH-no)* (sooner or later—they say "later or sooner"), you'll want to explore *las gangas (las GAHN-gahs)* (the bargains) in *abarrotes (ah-bar-RO-tays)* (groceries).

Don't be intimidated if you don't always know exactly what you're *comprando (kohm-PRAHN-doh)* (buying). A lot of *comida enlatada (ko-MEE-dah en-la-TAH-dah)* (canned food) can be identified by pictures on the label. And if you are adventurous, you can learn a little *español* and try something new for a very small *precio (PRAY-see-oh)* (price).

Canned *jugos de fruta (HOO-gos day FROO-tah)* (fruit juices) are usually a good buy. Aside from the common *jugo de durazno (HOO-go day doo-RAHS-no)* (peach nectar or juice), *piña (PEEN-yah)* (pineapple) or *toronja (toh-ROHN-ha)* (grapefruit), you'll find the more exotic *guayaba (gwy-AH-bah)* (guava) and *mango (MAHN-go)*. Your *diccionario (deek-see-oh-NAH-ree-oh)* (dictionary) will help you decipher more *sabores (sah-BOH-rays)* (flavors).

Fruta en bote (FROO-tah en BO-tay) (fruit in cans) is usually *en almíbar (en all-MEE-bar)* (in syrup). The *fruta* can be *entera (en-TAY-rah)* (whole) or *en rebanadas (en ray-bah-NAH-dahs)* (sliced, literally in slices). *Ate,* a Mexican product, is a paste made of various *frutas* and can be used like jam, but is not as sweet. *Mermelada (mair-may-LAH-dah)* (jam—it looks like marmalade, so it will be easy to remember) is also available to go with your *pan (pahn)* (bread). Other purely Mexican canned foods include *chongos (CHOHN-gos)*, a very sweet cheese that can be served "as is" for dessert, and *cascara de guayaba (KAHS-kah-rah day gwy-AH-bah) (guava shells)* which are great filled with *queso crema (KAY-so KRAY-ma)* (cream cheese), also called *queso filadélfia (KAY-so fee-lah-DAIL-fee-ah)* (Philadelphia cheese). The Mexican products don't have a translation in English, but can be an eating adventure.

The dairy case contains *leche (LAY-chay)* (milk), *yogurt (yo-GOORT)*, *queso* and *huevos (WAY-vos)* or *blanquillos (blahn-KEEY-yos)* (eggs—*blanquillos* is a slang expression but avoids *huevos* which has another meaning in slang, referring anatomically to certain parts of the male body).

Mexican *quesos* are very different from those you find in the States. Most are white or light yellow in color, because they do not add food coloring. Some *tiendas* will give you a *prueba (proo-WAY-bah)* (taste). Or you can experiment by *comprando* a small quantity of several *quesos*. You might ask if it is *blando (BLAHN-doh)* (soft) *o duro (oh*

DOO-ro) (or hard). Some of the *quesos duros* are so hard that they must be grated and sprinkled on food like Parmesan cheese.

La carne (la KAR-nay) (meat) is another *ganga.* Whether you prefer *res (rays)* (beef), *carne de puerco (PWAYR-ko)* (pork), *cordero (kor-DAY-ro)* (lamb) or *pollo (POY-yoh)* (chicken), the *supermercado* has it. If you're going to make hamburgers, get some *carne molida (KAR-nay mo-LEE-dah)* (ground beef). Mexican *carne* is frequently cut differently than American meat. It's a good idea to tell *el carnicero (el kar-nee-SAY-ro)* (the butcher) what you plan to do with the meat. He'll give you the best cut for your purposes. *Carne para asar (PA-rah ah-SAR)* (meat to broil or cook on the barbecue) is not necessarily *bifstek (beef-STAYK)* (steak). You can get *carne para hacer caldo (PA-rah ah-SAIR KALL-doh)* (soup meat) *con hueso (kohn WAY-so)* (with bone) or *sin hueso (seen WAY-so).* If you want *chuletas (choo-LAY-tahs)* (chops), you can have them cut *delgadas (dail-GAH-dahs)* (thin) or *gruesas (groo-WAY-sahs)* (thick).

There are *gangas* on *jabón (ha-BOHN)* (soap) and on *galletas (gy-YEH-tahs)* (cookies or crackers). If you can't find something, ask: *"¿Dónde está _____?"* *(DOHN-day es-TAH)* (where is?). For example, *¿Dónde está la leche? (DOHN-day es-TAH la LAY-chay)* (where is the milk?) for a singular item. *¿Dónde están las especias? (DOHN-day es-TAHN las es-PAY-see-ahs)* (where are the spices?) for plural items. With *diccionario* in hand, you can have an *abarrote* adventure.

Chapter 11

Seafood...
Los Mariscos

Because Mexico has an extremely long coastline, some of the freshest seafood in the world is served there. Several towns even hold contests for local restaurants to compete in preparing the tastiest and most eye-appealing dishes based on fish and shellfish. Even a short trip to Baja reveals that most eateries feature several seafood dishes along with the predictable *enchiladas* and combination plates.

When ordering in a dining room, you will need a certain amount of menu Spanish. This is made easier because many restaurants have bilingual *cartas (KAR-tahs)* (menus). You can refresh your memory before ordering by cross checking the English side. *Meseros (meh-SAY-ros)* (waiters) are particularly patient people who will humor you if you insist on *ordenando (or-day-NAHN-doh)* (ordering) in Spanish. This is good practice, even if they correct your pronunciation. You can further insure that you get the item you want by pointing to the *menú (may-NOO)* (menu) at the same time you pronounce the dish, important for beginners and picky eaters.

A *pez (pehs)* (fish) is what swims in the sea. Fish that has been caught and is intended for eating is referred to as *pescado (pehs-KAH-doh)*. This refers only to our finned friends of the deep. You can generally choose your favorite method of preparation including *frito (FREE-toh)* (fried), *a la parrilla (ah la par-REE-yah)* (grilled or broiled), *al mojo de ajo (all MO-ho day AH-ho)* (sauteed in garlic butter), *en mantequilla (en mahn-tay-KEE-yah)* (in butter), or *a la Veracruzana (ah la bay-rah-kroo-SAH-nah)* (Veracruz-style, in a sauce of tomato, chile and onions).

To order your fish you say, *"Favor de darme _____"* *(fah-VOR day DAR-may)* (please give me _____). You fill in the blank with the fish and how you want it prepared. For example, *"Favor de darme pescado a la parrilla"* (please give me grilled fish). Notice that the method of cooking goes after the fish. When the fish is served whole, it is called *entero (en-TAY-ro)*. When a filet is served, it is *filete de pescado (fee-LAY-tay day pes-KAH-doh)*. You may want to specify which you prefer. Or *el mesero* may ask you.

All the other goodies from the sea which we love to eat fall in the category of *mariscos (ma-REES-kos)* (shellfish). This includes the ever-popular *langosta (lawn-GO-stah)* (lobster) *al estilo Puerto Nuevo (all es-TEE-lo PWAYR-toh noo-WAY-vo)* (Newport-style, named for a fishing town in Baja famous for lobster dinners) or *al vapor (all vah-POR)* (steamed).

Other favorites are *camarón (kah-ma-ROHN)* (shrimp), *abulón (ah-boo-LOHN)* (abalone), *almejas (all-MAY-has)* (clams), *pulpo (POOL-po)* (octopus) and *jaiba (HY-bah)* or *cangrejo (kahn-GRAY-ho)* (crab). These can be *empanizados (em-pa-nee-SAH-dohs)* (breaded), *al mojo de ajo* (like the fish above), or in *cockteles (kohk-TAY-lays)* (seafood cocktails).

If you are **preocupado** *(pray-oh-koo-PA-doh)* (worried—end it with an "a" if you are a woman) that a dish will be too spicy or hot, ask: *"¿Es picante?" (es pee-KAHN-tay)* (is it spicy/hot?). Or simply say: *"¿Pica?" (PEE-kah)* (Is it hot? or, literally, does it sting?).

When you want to express your delight with the food, say: *"¡Sabroso! (sah-BRO-so)* (delicious). Or just say, *"¡Que rico!" (kay REE-ko)* (how rich). Remember that practicing your new words frequently will make them part of your vocabulary. They will be easier to remember the more you use them. And while you savor the delights of a **marisco** dinner, or any other meal, *"¡Buen provecho!" (bwayn pro-VAY-cho)* (enjoy).

Chapter 12

Cooking ....
Cocinar

If you consider yourself a gourmet *chef (chayf—*not *shef,* as in English) (chef), you may want to try out some of the recipes you find in Latin American magazines or cookbooks. Or *quisás (kee-SAHS)* (maybe) you have a Spanish-speaking *cocinera (ko-see-NAY-rah)* (cook, feminine) with whom you want to communicate better. So this chapter deals with *cocinar (ko-see-NAR)* (cooking, literally, "to cook"— frequently in Spanish the infinitive is used when we would use the gerund in English). So get out your *mandiles (mahn-DEE-lays)* (aprons) and *sartenes (sar-TEN-ays)* (frying pans) and let's go to *la cocina (la ko-SEE-nah)* (the kitchen).

Almost anyone can *hervir agua (air-VEER AH-gwah)* (boil water). But if you want to *freír (fray-EER)* (to fry) up something good, like *pollo frito (POY-yo FREE-toh)* (fried chicken), you need a little skill, and some *hierbas (YAIR-bahs)* (herbs) and *especias (es-PAY-see-ahs)* (spices).

First you are going to **derretir** *(dair-ray-TEER)* (to melt) the **manteca** *(mahn-TAY-kah)* (shortening or lard—to ensure that you get vegetable shortening ask for **manteca vegetal)**. Una receta *(OO-nah ray-SAY-tah)* (a recipe; the same word means prescription) might say something like this: **La gallina** *(la guy-YEE-nah)* (the chicken) **partida en trozos** *(par-TEE-dah en TRO-sos)* (cut in pieces) **se lava bien** *(say LA-vah bee-EN)* (is washed well) **con agua fría** *(kohn AH-gwah FREE-ah)* (with cold water). You will **dar una capa** *(dar OO-nah KAH-pa)* (coat, literally "give a coating") to each **trozo** with **harina** *(ah-REE-nah)* (flour) or **pan molido** *(pahn mo-LEE-doh)* (bread crumbs) **mezclado** *(mays-KLAH-doh)* (mixed) with **hierbas** before you begin to **freír**.

If you prefer, you can **hornear** *(or-nay-AR)* (bake) **el pollo.** You will put it in **un trasto refractario** *(oon TRAH-sto ray-frahk-TAH-ree-oh)* (a baking dish) which has been **engrasado** *(en-grah-SAH-doh)* (greased). **Las recetas** frequently do not give a **temperatura** *(tem-pay-rah-TOO-rah)* (temperature) but will say, **"en el horno** *(en el OR-no)* (in the oven) **a fuego lento"** *(ah FWAY-go LEN-toh)* (at a low temperature, or literally "with a slow fire") or **"a fuego vivo"** *(ah FWAY-go VEE-vo)* (a fast or lively fire). Many ovens in Latin America do not have temperature gauges, so **las cocineras** just approximate.

The same expressions are used to **cocinar en la estufa** *(en la es-TOO-fah)* (on the stove). **Otra receta** *(OH-trah)* (another) may indicate to **agregar** *(ah-gray-GAR)* (to add) **un diente de ajo** *(oon dee-EN-tay day AH-ho)* (a clove of garlic, literally a "tooth" of garlic) **picado** *(pee-KAH-doh)* (chopped or minced) and **maizena** *(ma-ee-SAY-nah)* (corn starch, a brand name). **Dejar hervir** *(day-HAR air-VEER)* (let it boil) **a fuego regular** *(ah FWAY-go ray-goo-LAR)* (over a medium fire) until it is **espeso** *(es-PAY-so)* (thick, used to refer to liquids). Be sure to **mover** *(mo-VAIR)* (to stir) while **cocinando** *(ko-see-NAHN-doh)* (cooking) so it won't stick to the **sartén.** If a **temperatura** is given, it is usually in **centígrado** *(sen-TEE-grah-doh)* (centigrade). Here are some common **temperaturas de hornear** and their equivalent in Fahrenheit:

150 grados C = 300 degrees F
180 grados C = 350 degrees F
200 grados C = 400 degrees F
260 grados C = 500 degrees F

Choosing *una olla (OO-nah OY-yah)* (a pot) or *una cacerola (OO-nah kah-say-RO-la)* (a casserole or pan) is easy. But *medir (may-DEER)* (to measure) in Spanish means thinking metric. Most people can remember that a *kilo (KEE-lo)* (kilo) is *2.2 libras (LEE-brahs)* (pounds) and a *litro (LEE-tro)* (liter) is a little more than a quart. A 250 milliliter measure replaces the English 8 ounce cup. For a *cucharada (koo-cha-RAH-dah)* (tablespoon) use 15 milliliters, and for a *cucharita (koo-cha-REE-tah)* (teaspoon) use a 5 milliliter measure for accuracy.

This is only a taste of the myriad of cooking terms. If you didn't know how to cook before, then this chapter will not make you a master *cocinero* in any language. But keep practicing and you'll have fun *en español en la cocina.* If you're serious about *cocinando en español,* get **Bilingual Cooking:** *La Cocina Bilingüe,* by Elizabeth Reid (see the order form at the back of this book), a Spanish/English cookbook.

Chapter 13

Painless Spanish: Español Sin Dolor

There are a lot of words which are written almost the
same in both *inglés* and *español*, called cognates. This
is a practically *sin dolor (seen doh-LOR)* (painless)
method of *aumentando (ow-men-TAHN-doh)* (enlarging or
augmenting) your *vocabulario (vo-kah-boo-LA-ree-oh)* (vocabulary). Remember, *la pronunciación (la pro-NOON-see-
ah-see-OHN)* (the pronunciation) will be very different, so
it is *importante (eem-por-TAHN-tay)* (important) to practice

saying and listening to these *palabras (pa-LA-bras)* (words). Many words add a final vowel or change the silent "e" in English to a vowel. You already know the meaning of these *palabras* so here is how *la pronunciación* goes in Spanish:

caso (KAH-so) case
causa (KOW-sah) cause
costo (KO-sto) cost
dentista (den-TEE-sta) dentist
evidente (eh-vee-DEN-tay) evident
exclusivo (ex-kloo-SEE-vo) exclusive
favorito (fah-vo-REE-toh) favorite
figura (fee-GOO-rah) figure
líquido (LEE-kee-doh) liquid
lista (LEE-stah) list
literatura (lee-tay-rah-TOO-rah) literature
mapa (MA-pa) map
medicina (may-dee-SEE-nah) medicine
minuto (mee-NOO-toh) minute
moderno (mo-DAIR-no) modern
música (MOO-see-kah) music
nota (NO-tah) note
parte (PAR-tay) part
persona (pair-SO-nah) person
portero (por-TAY-ro) porter
práctica (PRAK-tee-kah) practice
problema (pro-BLAY-ma) problem
producto (pro-DOOK-toh) product
restaurante (rest-ow-RAHN-tay) restaurant
rosa (RO-sah) rose
tubo (TOO-bo) tube
uso (OO-so) use

If the word in English begins with an "s." there will be an "e" before it in Spanish:

espacio (es-PA-see-oh) space
especial (es-PAY-see-ALL) special

> *espíritu (es-PEE-ree-too)* spirit
> *estación (es-tah-see-OHN)* station
> *estado (es-TAH-doh)* state
> *estilo (es-TEE-lo)* style

And if *la palabra* has a double consonant in *inglés*, there will be only one in *español*:

> *antena (ahn-TEN-ah)* antenna
> *anual (ahn-WALL)* annual
> *comercial (ko-mair-see-ALL)* commercial
> *imposible (eem-po-SEE-blay)* impossible
> *intelectual (een-tay-layk-TWALL)* intellectual
> *inteligible (een-tay-lay-HEE-blay)* intelligible
> *ocasional (oh-kah-see-oh-NALL)* occasional
> *oficial (oh-fee-see-ALL)* official
> *posible (po-SEE-blay)* possible
> *profesional (pro-fay-see-oh-NALL)* professional

As with all easy things, you have to be careful. There are some *palabras* to watch out for—they look similar to the English equivalent, but have meanings radically different. Study this *lista* and remember the meanings, as well as how to pronounce them.

> *falta (FALL-tah)* lack of something, **not** fault
> *idioma (ee-dee-OH-ma)* language, **not** idiom
> *largo (LAR-go)* long, **not** large
> *lectura (layk-TOO-rah)* reading, **not** lecture
> *letra (LAYT-rah)* letter of the alphabet, **not** mail
> *librería (lee-bray-REE-ah)* bookstore, **not** library
> *molestar (mo-lay-STAR)* to bother, **not** to molest
> *pan (pahn)* bread, **not** a pan
> *pariente (pa-ree-EN-tay)* a relative, **not** a parent
> *realizar (ray-ah-lee-SAR)* to take place or attain, **not** to realize

Fortunately the list of words that look the same and truly are the same is *mucho más largo (MOO-cho mas LAR-go)* (much longer) than the list of tricky words that are not what they seem to be. There is an advantage for those *personas* who are not careful spellers in *inglés*—they may already be writing the *palabras* as they appear in *español*. Of course, *la pronunciación* is everything, so don't be neglectful in studying *el idioma. La falta de práctica* is no excuse. Try inventing sentences using the words from these lists, then say the sentences out loud several times for the pronunciation. This can be both fun and funny. For example:

> *El costo es la causa evidente de su producto favorito.*
> *El estilo moderno del restaurante es profesional y exclusivo.*
> *La literatura es parte de la lectura intelectual en la librería.*
> *Con el antena especial es posible realizar un minuto inteligible.*

Get together with a friend and see who can make a sentence using the most words from the list. The prize is a bigger vocabulary.

Chapter 14

Weather ....

El Tiempo

With the change of **estaciones** *(eh-stah-see-OH-nays)* (seasons), frequently comes a change of **tiempo** *(tee-EM-po)* (weather). And, since everyone talks about the weather, it is a good idea to add some weather words to your Spanish vocabulary. **Bienvenidos otoño,** *(bee-en-vay-NEE-dohs oh-TOHN-yo)* (welcome autumn), **adiós verano** *(ah-dee-OHS vay-RAH-no)* (goodbye summer).

Whereas in English we say, "It is sunny," in Spanish we use the verb **hacer** *(ah-SAYR)* (to make or do) to describe meteorologic activity. "It is sunny," translates to, *"Hace sol"* *(AH-say sol)* (literally, it makes sun). The word **caliente** *(kah-lee-EN-tay)* (hot) refers to **agua** *(AH-gwah)* (water) or other heated things. It is not used to speak about **el tiempo.**

The word *calor (kah-LOR)* (literally heat) describes a hot day; so, *"Hace calor" (AH-say kah-LOR)* is the way to say "It is hot" if you are talking about the weather. We experience a lot of *calor* when we have *un cielo despejado (oon see AY lo des-pay-HA-doh)* (a clear sky) in *el verano. Otoño* is the time when leaves *caen (KY-en)* (fall). It is also the beginning of *la temporada de fútbol americano (la tem-po-RAH-dah day FOOT-bowl ah-may-ree-KAH-no)* (football season).

When *el invierno (el een-vee-AIR-no)* (the winter) comes, *hace frío (AH-say FREE-oh)* (it's cold). Sometimes we have *nubes (NOO-bays)* (clouds) or *neblina (nay-BLEE-nah)* (fog). In *las montañas (las mohn-TAHN-yahs)* (the mountains) and in *los climas fríos (los KLEE-mas FREE-ohs)* (the cold climates) you find *la nieve (la nee-AY-vay)* (snow). Some people like it to *nevar (nay-VAR)* (to snow). But *no hace mucho frío (no AH-say MOO-cho FREE-oh)* (it's not very cold) in most of *México.* If you like *nieve,* you won't find much there, except the kind you eat *(it also means ice cream).*

La primavera (la pree-ma-VAY-rah) (spring) is my favorite *estación.* After *las tormentas (las tor-MEN-tahs)* (the storms) of winter, *el tiempo* begins to *calentar (kah-len-TAR)* (to warm up). Of course we have *la lluvia (la YOO-vee-ah)* (rain) occasionally. The verb to rain is *llover (yo-VAIR).* In the present tense this is conjugated as *llueve (yoo-WAY-vay) (it* rains) or *está lloviendo (es-TAH yo-vee-EN-doh)* (it is raining). In the past tense *llover* becomes *llovió (yo-vee-OH)* (it rained). This turns some streets to *lodo (LO-doh)* (mud) but it makes *el desierto (el deh-see-AIR-toh)* (the desert) bloom.

La primavera can also bring *el viento (el vee-EN-toh)* or *el aire (el I-ray)* (the wind). But that is just so that we can fly our *papelotes (pa-pay-LO-tays)* or *cometas (ko-MAY-tahs)* (kites). A light *brisa (BREE-sah)* (breeze) can be *refrescante (ray-fray-SKAHN-tay)* (refreshing). *(Brisa* sometimes refers to *neblina* in *México.)* Soon *verano* returns with *calor* and *tormentas electricas (tor-MEN-tahs eh-LAYK-tree-kahs)* (thunder storms). A summer evening watching *los relámpagos* *(los ray-LAHM-pa-gos)* (the lightening) and hearing *los truenos* *(los troo-WAY-nos)* (the thunder) is *espectacular* *(es-payk-tah-koo-LAR)* (spectacular). By the way, *"Tenemos buen tiempo,"* *(teh-NAY-mos bwayn tee-EM-po)* means "We are having good weather," **not** that we are having a good time. If you want to say, "we are enjoying ourselves," it is: *"Nos divertimos"* *(nos dee-vair-TEE-mos)*. Spanish has a verb just for "to have fun"—*divertirse* *(dee-vair-TEER-say)*.

A comment on *el tiempo* is easy to work into a conversation and makes a great opener. So, now that you have studied these words, talk about the weather. Even if no one does anything about it.

Chapter 15

Winter:
Invierno

I**nvierno** *(een-vee-AIR-no)* (winter) is the ***temporada***
(tem-po-RAH-dah) (season) for so many things: watching
***ballenas** (by-YAY-nahs)* (whales), ***ir de compras** (eer day
KOHM-prahs)* (going shopping), and ***pachangas** (pa-
CHAHN-gahs)* (blow-out parties). If you have ever taken ***un
viaje** (oon vee-AH-hay)* (a trip) down to ***Ojo de Liebre*** Bay
(OH-ho day lee-AY-bray) (the name of the bay is "eye of the
hare" and it is near Guerrero Negro), then you really have
***unos cuentos** (OO-nos KWAYN-tohs)* (some stories) to tell.
Las ballenas are ***tan gigantescos** (tahn hee-gahn-TAYS-kos)*
(so huge)! Only during ***el invierno*** in Baja do you have such
a good chance to see them ***de cerca** (day SAIR-kah)* (up
close).

Except for those with special permits, ***un barco** (oon
BAR-ko)* (a boat) is ***prohibido** (pro-ee-BEE-doh)* (prohib-
ited) in ***las bahías** (las bah-EE-ahs)* (the bays) where the
ballenas are calving. (Remember that the "h" is silent when

you pronounce these words). That is because the *ballenas* are *protegidas (pro-tay-HEE-dahs)* (protected). They are also dangerous for small craft!

If you aren't going *ballena*-watching, then you probably will be *comprando regalos (kohm-PRAHN-doh ray-GAH-los)* for your *familia (fah-MEE-lee-ah)* (family) and *amistades (ah-mee-STAH-days)* (friends). There never seems to be *suficiente (soo-fee-see-EN-tay)* (enough) time to prepare for *los días festivos (los DEE-ahs fes-TEE-vos)* (the holidays). Notice that you use *suficiente* when you mean enough. *Bastante (bahs-TAHN-tay)* means "enough" but it also implies too much or a lot.

In addition to *ir de compras*, you'll want to *ir al mandado (eer al mahn-DAH-doh)* (to go grocery shopping) to have on hand *bastante comida (bah-STAHN-tay ko-MEE-dah)* (plenty of food) for *invitados (een-vee-TAH-dohs)* (guests) and *visitas (vee-SEE-tahs)* (visitors). *Tal vez (tall vays)* (perhaps) someone in your home will *hornear (or-nay-AR)* (bake) *unas galletas (OO-nahs guy-YEH-tahs)* (some cookies) or *un pastel (oon PA-stayl)* (a cake). If you begin early with all of these preparations, then you'll be *listo (LEE-sto; ends with an "a" for the ladies)* (ready) to party when guests drop in.

There are various degrees of party in Mexico, from the polite *reunión (ray-oo-nee-OHN)* (gathering), to the moderate *fiesta (fee-AY-stah)*, to the somewhat rowdy *pachanga*. The word *"parti"* is being used by many *jovenes (HO-vay-nays)* (young people) in the *frontera (frohn-TAY-rah)* (border area) instead of *fiesta*. They borrowed it from *inglés*.

Con suerte (kohn SWAYR-tay) (with luck) you'll be invited to a *fiesta* where there will be *las posadas (las po-SAH-dahs)*. This Mexican tradition re-enacts the search of *José y María* (Joseph and Mary) for *posada* (lodging) in *Belén (bay-LEN)* (Bethlehem) (see chapter 17 and appendix A for more information). The *posada* can be done inside one house, going *de cuarto a cuarto (day KWAHR-toh ah KWAHR-toh)* (from room to room), or it can be done in a *colónia (ko-LO-nee-ah)* (neighborhood) going *de casa a casa (day KAH-sah ah KAH-sah)* (from house to house). The group with *José* and *María cantan (KAHN-tahn)* (sing, conjugated for "they") a request for *posada*. They are turned down everywhere until finally someone representing the inn keeper allows them to enter. Once the group is allowed in, the *fiesta* begins in earnest. This is a quaint Mexican tradition and it's fun to observe, as well.

Chapter 16

Christmas: *La Navidad*

W hen there is a chill in the air and the stores are all decorated, you can't help but begin to think about *la Navidad (la nah-vee-DAHD)* (Christmas). Of course, *la Navidad* is not just the material side of giving *regalos (ray-GAH-los)* (gifts). *Reunirse (ray-oo-NEER-say)* (getting together) *con familia y amigos (kohn fah-MEE-lee-ah ee ah-MEE-gos)* (with family and friends) is a big part of celebrating on either side of the border.

If you are fortunate enough to be *invitado (een-vee-TAH-doh)* (invited) to the home of a Mexican family *para celebrar (PA-rah say-lay-BRAR)* (to celebrate), you will note some differences in seasonal decorations. While some may have *un árbol (oon AR-bowl)* (a tree) this custom is borrowed from the United States (and from Germany before that). The important decoration for a Mexican home is a *nacimiento (nah-see-mee-EN-toh)* (nativity scene) whose figures may be family heirlooms. The *nacimiento* is displayed with *orgullo (or-GOO-yo)* (pride) and *amor (ah-MOR)* (love). *El niño Jesus (el NEEN-yo hay-SOOS)* (the baby Jesus) is not added to the scene until *la Noche Buena (la NO-chay BWAY-nah)* (Christmas eve; literally the good night).

Nochebuena is also the Spanish word for the poinsettia flower whose flaming blossoms gave rise to *una leyenda (OO-nah lay-EN-dah)* (a legend). *Un chico pobre (oon CHEE-ko PO-bray)* (a poor boy) wanted to take a *regalo* to *el niño Jesus* at *la iglesia (la ee-GLAY-see-ah)* (the church). He gathered branches of *hojas verdes (OH-has VAIR-days)* (green leaves) while the other children mocked him for not having an appropriate present.

But when he arrived at *la iglesia, un milagro (oon mee-LA-grow)* (a miracle) had taken place. Each branch was topped with a brilliant red, star-shaped flower—*un regalo muy apto (MOO-ee AHP-toh)* (very appropriate)! *El chico pobre* presented his *regalo con orgullo* beside *los pastores (los pa-STO-rays)* (the shepherds) and *los Reyes Magos (los RAY-ays MA-gos)* (the kings or wisemen) in *el nacimiento.*

Los Reyes Magos, also known as *los Santos Reyes, (los SAHN-tohs RAY-ays)* are the ones who bring the gifts in Mexico, although Santa Claus often visits, too. The kings come on January 6th. This is the Anglo-Saxon Epiphany or twelfth day of Christmas. Since *Navidad* is celebrated from December 14th, when *las posadas (las po-SAH-dahs)* begin (see chapter 17), to January 6th, *la celebración (la say-lay-brah-see-OHN)* (the celebration) is a little later in Mexico than in *los Estados Unidos (eh-STAH-dohs oo-NEE-dohs)* (the United States).

So keep in the Christmas spirit. And remember: *No deben de hacer pucheros (no DAY-ben day ah-SAIR poo-CHAY-ros)* (you better not pout) *y no deben de llorar (ee no DAY-ben day yo-RAR)* (and you better not cry). Everyone you meet will greet you with, *"¡Feliz Navidad!" (fay-LEES nah-vee-DAHD)* (merry Christmas) *y próspero Año Nuevo (ee PROS-pay-ro AHN-yo noo-WAY-vo)* (and a prosperous New Year). And now you can wish them the same.

Chapter 17

Lodging: *Las Posadas*

In Mexico one of the beautiful **costumbres** *(ko-STOOM-brays)* (customs) of *la* **Navidad** *(la nah-vee-DAHD)* (Christmas) is *las* **Posadas** *(las po-SAH-dahs)* (literally, the lodgings), a re-enactment of Joseph and Mary's arrival in Bethlehem and their search for a room. For the ten days preceding Christmas *Las Posadas* are staged all over Mexico in small **pueblos** *(PWAY-blos)* (towns) with the church as the center of activity, and in large **ciudades** *(see-oo-DAH-days)* (cities) both in private homes going around the **colónia** *(ko-LO-nee-AH)* (neighborhood) and at the cathedrals.

Anyone may participate in the public *Posadas*—but be prepared to **cantar** *(kahn-TAR)* (to sing)! The people accompany *José* (Joseph) and *María* (Mary) and begin by singing a plea for shelter at a specific door:

¿Quién les da posada (kee-EN lays dah po-SAH-dah)
(Who will give shelter)
A estos peregrinos (ah ES-tos pay-ray-GREE-nos)
(To these pilgrims)
Que vienen cansados (kay vee-EN-en kahn-SAH-dohs)
(Who come tired)
De andar los caminos? (day ahn-DAR los ka-MEE-nos)
(From walking the roads?)

    El Posadero (el po-sah-DAY-ro) (the inn keeper), who is predesignated, will deny the request in formal Castilian (note the use of the *vosotros* form):

Por más que digáis (por mas kay dee-GUYS)
(No matter what you say)
Que venís rendidos (kay vay-NEES ren-DEE-dos)
(That you come exhausted)
No damos posada (no DAH-mos po-SAH-dah)
(We don't give lodging)
A desconocidos (ah days-ko-no-SEE-dohs)
(To strangers.)

    The people and *José* renew their request:

En nombre del cielo (en NOHM-bray dayl see-AY-lo)
(In the name of heaven)
Os pido posada (os PEE-doh po-SAH-dah)
(I ask you for shelter)
Pues no puede andar (pways no PWAY-day ahn-DAR)
(Unable to walk is)
Ya mi esposa amada (yah mee es-PO-sah ah-MA-dah)
(My beloved wife.)

    Heartless, *El Posadero* makes this reply:

Aquí no es mesón (ah-kee no es may-SOHN)
(This is not an inn)
Sigan adelante (SEE-gan ah-day-LAHN-tay)
(Continue on)
Yo no puedo abrir (yo no PWAY-doh ah-BREER)

(I cannot open)
*No sea algún tunante (no SAY-ah all-GOON
too-NAHN-tay)* (Don't be a vagrant.)

José and the people implore once more:

No seas inhumano (no SAY-ahs een-oo-MA-no)
(Don't be inhuman)
Y ten caridad (ee ten kah-ree-DAHD)
(And have charity)
*Que el Dios de los cielos (kay el dee-OHS day los
see-AY-los)*
(And God in heaven)
Te lo premiará (tay lo pray-mee-ah-RAH)
(Will reward you.)

El Posadero finally runs them off with:

Ya se pueden ir (yah say PWAY-den eer)
(You can go now)
Y no molestar (ee no mo-lay-STAR)
(And stop bothering me)
Porque si me enfado (por-KAY see may en-FA-doh)
(Because if I get mad)
Los voy a apalear (los voy ah ah-pa-lay-AR)
(I'm going to beat you with a stick.)

Here *José, María* and the people move on to another
home where the verses are repeated. After several unsuc-
cessful attempts, they reach a house where they sing the
previous verses, but add:

Venimos rendidos (vay-NEE-mos ren-DEE-dohs)
(We come exhausted)
Desde Nazaret (DES-day nah-sah-RET)
(From Nazareth)
Yo soy carpintero (yo soy kar-peen-TAY-ro)
(I am a carpenter)
De nombre José (day NOHM-bray ho-SAY)
(By the name of Joseph.)

The stubborn *Posadero* still does not give in to their request:

No me importa su nombre
(No may eem-POR-ta soo NOHM-bray)
(Your name is not important to me)
Déjenme dormir (Day-hen-may dor-MEER)
(Let me sleep)
Pues que ya les digo (pways kay yah lays DEE-go)
(I've already told you)
Que no hemos de abrir (kay no AY-mos day ah-BREER)
(That we won't open up.)

The people and *José* entreat the *Posadero*, who is softening:

Mi esposa es María (mee es-PO-sah es ma-REE-ah)
(My wife is Mary)
La reina del cielo (la RAY-nah del see-AY-lo)
(The queen of heaven)
Madre va a ser (MA-dray vah ah sair)
(She's going to be the mother)
Del divino Verbo (del dee-VEE-no VAIR-bo)
(Of the divine Word.)

At last, recognizing his distinguished guests, the *Posadero* relents, apologizing to them:

¿Eres tú José? (AY-rays too ho-SAY)
(Are you Joseph?)
¿Y tu esposa María? (ee too es-PO-sah ma-REE-ah)
(And your wife is Mary?)
Entren, peregrinos (EN-tren pay-ray-GREE-nos)
(Come in, pilgrims)
No los conocía (no los ko-no-SEE-ah)
(I didn't know you.)

In spite of their ordeal, *José* and the people sing a blessing on the house:

Dichosa esta casa (dee-CHO-sah ES-tah KAH-sah)
(Blessed be this house)
Que nos da posada (kay nos dah po-SAH-dah)
(That gives us lodging)
Dios siempre le dé (dee-OHS see-EM-pray lay day)
(May God always give you)
Su dicha sagrada (soo DEE-cha sah-GRAH-dah)
(His holy blessing.)

EL Posadero now welcomes them in:

Posada os damos (po-SAH-dah os DAH-mos)
(Lodging we give you)
Con mucha alegría (kohn MOO-cha ah-lay-GREE-ah)
(With much happiness)
Entra, José justo (EN-trah ho-SAY HOO-stoh)
(Come in, Joseph the just)
Entra con María (EN-trah kohn ma-REE-ah)
(Come in with Mary.)

This little folk opera takes place all over Latin America in December. Practice the lines of the people and *José* a few times and you'll be ready. You can hope for an invitation to a private *Posada,* or seek out the one given at the local church. If you are too shy to sing along, at least you will know what they are saying.

Chapter 18

Health.....
La Salúd

What do you do if you find yourself a bit **raquítico** *(rah-KEE-tee-ko)* (feeble, under the weather) while south of the border? There's no need to high-tail it back to the states. Simply consult some of the well-qualified local medical personnel. You may choose to seek out **un médico** *(oon MAY-dee-ko)* (a doctor, not a medic) or describe your symptoms to **un farmacólogo** *(oon far-ma-KO-lo-go)* (a pharmacist) at the corner **botica** *(bo-TEE-ka)* (drug store).

Whether you have **una herida** *(OO-nah ay-REE-dah)* (a wound or injury) or a touch of **diarrea** *(dee-ar-RAY-ah)* (diarrhea), help is not far away. Or, perhaps you know someone who has been **celebrando** *(say-lay-BRAWN-doh)* (celebrating) a little bit more than **lo que el cuerpo aguanta** *(lo kay el KWAYR-po ah-GWAHN-tah)* (that which the body will endure). He may have even greeted **el Día del Año**

Nuevo (el DEE-ah del AHN-yo noo-WAY-vo) (New Year's Day) with *la cruda (la KROO-dah)* (a hangover—that's an easy one to remember!).

Telling the *farmacólogo* or *médico* where it hurts is of primary importance: *me duele la espalda (may DWAY-lay la es-PALL-dah)* (my back hurts te that). No parts of the body are referred to as *el* or *la* (the), not *mi (mee)* (my). *Me duele el hombro (may DWAY-lay el OHM-bro)* (my shoulder hurts). Be careful with those final vowels—*hombre* is man and *hombro* is shoulder. The verb *doler (doh-LAIR)* is to ache or to hurt. *Me duele el pecho (may DWAY-lay el PAY-cho)* is literally, my chest hurts me. If you are speaking on behalf of someone else say, *"Le duele la cabeza" (lay DWAY-lay la kah-BAY-sah)* (his or her head hurts).

To say that you hurt yourself, use the verb *lastimar (la-stee-MAR)* (to injure). *Me lastimé el pie (may la-stee-MAY el PEE-ay)* (I hurt my foot). Or, *me lastimé la pierna (May la-stee-MAY la pee-AIR-nah)* (I hurt my leg). *Me lastimé* is in the past tense. If speaking about someone else it's, *"Se lastimó el brazo" (say la-stee-MO el BRAH-so)* (he or she hurt his/her arm—it's the same for both sexes).

If you have an unfortunate accident at *la fogata (la fo-GAH-tah)* (the campfire) then you might say, *"Me quemé la mano" (may kay-MAY la MA-no)* (I burned my hand). However if you experience a burning sensation use the verb *arder (ar-DAIR). Me arden los ojos (may AR-den los OH-hos) (my eyes burn)*.

Got an itch? *Tengo comezón (TEN-go ko-may-SOHN)* (I have itching). Here it is *tiene comezón (tee-EN-ay ko-may-SOHN)* (he/she has itching) if you are telling about someone else's problem. Mother always said, *"¡No te rasques!" (no tay RAHS-kays)* (don't scratch).

If all else fails, when *el médico* asks, *"Dónde tiene dolor?" (DOHN-day tee-EH-nay doh-LOR)* (Where does it hurt?), you can point. He may write you *una receta (OO-nah ray-SAY-tah)* (a prescription) for *una inyección (OO-nah een-yek-see-OHN)* (a shot) or *unas pastillas (OO-nahs pa-STEE-yas)* (some pills). If you are *enfermo (en-FAIR-mo)* (sick—*enferma* for the ladies) *tome su medicina (TOH-may soo may-dee-SEE-nah)* (take your medicine).

Hopefully you will enjoy constant *buena salúd (BWAY-nah sah-LOOD)* (good health) and never have to use this vocabulary except to help others. But it is good to be prepared. By the way, if someone sneezes you say, *"Salúd."* And if they are ill, *"Ojalá que se mejore pronto"* (oh-ha-LA kay say may-HO-ray PRON-toh) (may you get well soon).

Chapter 19

Diet, Exercize
... Dieta y
Ejercicio

Do you sometimes make resolutions for **desarrollo personal** *(days-ar-ROY-yo pair-so-NALL)* (personal development or improvement)? If you are using your **fuerza de voluntad** *(FWAYR-sah day vo-loon-TAHD)* (will power) in **Latino América,** this chapter will give your vocabulary a boost with some helpful words.

Mucha gente *(MOO-cha HEN-tay)* (many people) go on **una dieta** *(OO-nah dee-AY-tah)* (a diet) as a form of **desarrollo personal.** If you enjoy **la comida de México** *(la ko-MEE-dah day MAY-hee-ko)* (the food of Mexico) it's easy to put on **unos kilitos demás** *(OO-nos kee-LEE-tos day-MAS)* (a few extra kilos, or a few extra pounds; remember, Mexico measures in metric). **Un programa de reducir**

peso (oon pro-GRAH-ma day ray-doo-SEER PAY-so) (a weight reduction program) will require a few new phrases to help with *la dieta.*

When someone offers you *el postre (el POS-tray)* (dessert), you can say: *"Estoy guardando la línea,"* *(es-TOY gwahr-DAHN-doh la LEE-nay-ah)* (I am watching my weight, or literally guarding the line). When confronted with rich dishes, *"Estoy contando las calorías,"* *(es-TOY kohn-TAHN-doh las kah-lo-REE-ahs)* (I am counting calories). Or simply say, *"No, gracias" (no GRAH-see-ahs)* (no, thanks). But be prepared to refuse more than once, since Mexican custom is for *el huésped (el WAYS-ped)* (the guest) to refuse what is offered until *el anfitrión (el ahn-fee-tree-OHN)* (the host) offers it three or more times. If your resistance to *la tentación (la ten-tah-see-OHN)* (temptation) is low, Mexican hospitality will sabotage *su dieta.*

Other *personas (pair-SO-nahs)* (persons, people) who are *dichosas (dee-CHO-sahs)* (fortunate) don't need to *contar las calorías (kohn-TAR las kah-lo-REE-ahs)* (to count calories). They may choose some other form of *desarrollo personal. Algunas (all-GOO-nahs)* (some) may begin *un programa de ejercicio (oon pro-GRAH-ma day eh-hair-SEE-see-oh)* (an exercise program). This is very good for *la salúd (la sah-LOOD)* (the health). They may choose to *correr (kor-RAIR)* (to run) or to *nadar (nah-DAR)* (to swim). If these seem *muy estrenuo (MOO-ee es-TRAY-noo-oh)* (very strenuous), then *caminar (kah-mee-NAR)* (walking) is another good choice. Many *médicos (MAY-dee-kos)* (doctors) recommend *el caminar* as a form of *ejercicio* that is *fácil (FAH-seel)* (easy), *barato (bah-RAH-toh)* (cheap) and needs no *equipo especial (ay-KEE-po es-peh-see-ALL)* (special equipment).

While *una dieta* and *ejercicio* are very popular forms of *desarrollo personal,* there are other possibilities. *Algunas personas* may resolve to *pasar más tiempo con la familia (pa-SAR mas tee-EM-po kohn la fah-MEE-lee-ah)* (spend more time with the family). Others will try to *pre-ocuparse menos (pray-oh-koo-PAR-say MAY-nos)* (worry less). Still others will strive to *adelantarse (ah-day-lahn-*

TAR-say) (to get ahead) **en el trabajo** *(en el trah-BAH-ho)* (at work) or **en la escuela** *(en la es-KWAY-la)* (at school). **Los estudiantes** *(los es-too-dee-AHN-tays)* (the students) will be working (we hope) for **buenas calificaciones** *(BWAY-nahs KAH-lee-fee-kah-see-OH-nays)* (good grades).

Some people will even choose to **aprender más español** *(ah-pren-DAIR mas es-pahn-YOL)* (to learn more Spanish). If **aprender el español** is your **meta** *(MAY-tah)* (goal), learn **una palabra** *(OO-nah pa-LA-brah)* (one word) each day and use it frequently. As you learn **nuevas palabras** *(noo-WAY-vahs pa-LA-brahs)* (new words), keep reviewing and using those words you learned **la semana pasada** *(la say-MA-nah pa-SAH-dah)* (last week, or the week past) and **el mes pasado** *(el mess pa-SAH-doh)* (last month). By the end of one year you will have expanded your vocabulary by 365 **palabras.** Not bad, and not too much **trabajo!**

Chapter 20

Beyond Mr. & Mrs. ————
Más Allá Que Sr. Y Sra.

When addressing people, we pretty much limit ourselves to the usual *Señor (sen-YOR)* (mister, abbreviated *Sr.*), and *Señora (sen-YO-rah)* (Mrs., abbreviated *Sra.*), and the occasional *doctor (dohk-TOR)* (doctor—*doctora, dohk-TOH-rah,* for a woman—abbreviated *Dr.* and *Dra.* respectively). However, in Spanish various titles are used when speaking about persons of particular professions and some are even used when speaking directly to the person. The abbreviations for these are used in writing, in place of Mr., Mrs., Ms., or Miss. These can be a real mystery to those who are learning Spanish. To unravel this mystery let's begin with your teacher.

Profesor (pro-fay-SOR) can be used when speaking to any male teacher; *profesora (pro-fay-SO-rah)* for a woman. It's true that *maestro (ma-ES-tro)* is one term in the dictionary, but this is a title of honor, similar to "professor" in English. It is rarely used with the *apellido (ah-pay-YEE-doh)* (last name). It would be correct to say, *"Profesora Vela, ¿qué significa esta palabra?" (kay sig-nee-FEE-kah ES-tah pa-la-bra)* (what does this word mean?). *Profe (PRO-fay)*, the shortened version may be used alone in a friendly way to refer directly or indirectly to a professor or to a studious person—it can even be *un apodo (oon ah-PO-doh)* (a nickname).

Licenciado (lee-sen-see-AH-doh, licenciada for a woman) may refer to an attorney, but it is a term of honor applied to anyone holding an advanced degree. *Abogado (ah-bo-GAH-doh)*, the other word meaning lawyer is not used this way. Thus, *"Buenos días, Licenciado Magallanes,"* would be a correct greeting for a scholar or political figure, as well as for an attorney. The abbreviation is *Lic.*, so *el correo (el ko-RAY-OH)* (the mail) would be addressed to *Lic. Magallanes.*

Ingeniero (een-hen-YAY-ro) (engineer) is also used when speaking to the person. The abbreviation is *Ing.* So, the greeting would be *"Me da gusto verlo, Ing. Moreno" (may dah GOO-sto VAIR-lo)* (how nice to see you, Ing. Moreno). Other mysteries when reading about people can be found in *C.P.* and *Arq. C.P.* is the abbreviation for *contador publico (kohn-tah-DOR POOB-lee-ko)* (public accountant) and is used in writing about a *C.P.* but not usually in speaking to him. Call him *"Señor"* or *"Licenciado." Arq.* stands for *arquitecto (ar-kee-TAYK-toh)* (architect) and substitutes for Mr. when speaking to or when writing about an architect. *"Gusto en verlo, Arq. Rubalcava,"*(Nice to see you, Arq. Rubalcava.)

While we are talking about abbreviations, *hermanos (air-MA-nos)* (brothers) is shortened to *hnos.* and is frequently used in the names of businesses. This abbreviation can really get you going if you don't know what it means. All sorts of words will almost fit: *honrado (ohn-RAH-doh)* (honored), *heno (AY-no)* (moss, hay), *hinchado (een-CHA-doh)* (swollen), *hondo (OHN-doh)* (deep), *hongo (OHN-go)* (mushroom), even *honesto (oh-NAY-sto)* (honest). But now you know that *Vila Hnos.* means "Vila Brothers" and not any of those other things.

Now that you know the correct form to use when addressing people of various professions, try to speak to people and you'll get more practice which really is the key to getting comfortable with a second language. Remember how hard it was to *amarrar sus zapatos (ah-mar-RAR soos sah-PA-tohs)* (tie your shoes) when you were first learning as a child? Now you can do it with your eyes closed. That's what practice and repetition can do for your *español.*

Chapter 21

Clothing . . . *La Ropa*

B uying *ropa (RO-pa)* (clothing) in **México** can be *muy divertido (MOO-ee dee-vair-TEE-doh)* (lots of fun). And you can *ahorrar (ah-or-RAR)* (save) *mucho dinero (MOO-cho dee-NAY-ro)* (a lot of money). But what if you find a little, out-of-the-way *tienda (tee-EN-dah)* (shop) where the clerk speaks *no inglés (een-GLAYS)* (English)? This chapter has phrases that will help you.

To express satisfaction you say, *"Me gusta_____" (may GOO-stah)* (I like _____, or literally _____ pleases me). So, **Me gusta esta blusa** *(may GOO-stah ES-tah BLOO-sah)* (I like this blouse), or **Me gusta esta playera** *(may GOO-stah ES-tah ply-AY-rah)* (I like this tee-shirt). As you know, some items are feminine and some are masculine. But this has nothing to do with which sex usually wears the article of *ropa.*

The above examples are feminine. If the item is masculine, you change "this" to *este: Me gusta este vestido (may GOO-stah ES-tay veh-STEE-doh)* (I like this dress). *Me gusta este chaleco (muy GOO-stah ES-tay cha-LAY-ko)* (I like this vest).

As in English, some pieces of clothing are referred to in the singular, i.e. *el abrigo (ah-BREE-go)* (overcoat), and some are referred to in the plural, *los zapatos (sah-PA-tohs)* (shoes). When an article of clothing is plural, you must add an "n" and an "s": *Me gustan estas botas (may GOO-stan ES-tahs BO-tahs)* (I like these boots). If the item is masculine you change this to these: *Me gustan estos calcetines (may GOO-stahn ES-tos kahl-say-TEE-nays)* (I like these socks); or, *Me gustan estos guantes (may GOO-stahn ES-tos GWAHN-tays)* (I like these gloves).

The same changes hold if you are referring to several items that please you. For example, *Me gustan estas faldas (may GOO-stahn ES-tahs FALL-dahs)* (I like these skirts). Just pay attention to whether the item is masculine or feminine, singular or plural, and you will be speaking perfect *español.* When you try on *ropa* and it is too big, you say, *"Es muy grande" (es MOO-ee GRAHN-day)* (it's too big). *Grande* stays the same when modifying either masculine: *un gorro grande (oon GOR-ro GRAHN-day)* (a big cap), or feminine: *una bata grande (OO-nah BAH-tah GRAHN-day)* (a big robe). If it's too small, *chico* ends in "a" if feminine or "o" if masculine. *El suéter es muy chico (el SWAY-tair es MOO-ee CHEE-ko)* (the sweater is too small). *La chaqueta es muy chica (la cha-KAY-tah es MOO-ee CHEE-kah)* (the jacket is very small).

If you really like something you might want to buy it, if the price is right. So you say, *"Cuánto cuesta_____?" (KWAHN-toh KWAY-stah)* (How much is _____?). *Cuánto cuesta esta chamarra? (KWAHN-toh KWAY-stah ES-tah cha-MAR-rah)* (how much is this jacket?). Use *cuesta* if the item is singular; if it's plural, *cuestan—Cuánto cuestan estas medias (KWAHN-toh KWAY-stahn ES-tahs MAY-dee-ahs)* (how much are these stockings?).

If the price seems high say, *"Es muy caro" (es MOO-ee KAH-ro)* (it's very expensive). The clerk may lower the price. Later, when you are telling your friends about your bargains, they may say, *"¡Que barato!" (kay bah-RAH-toh)* (how cheap). When you have decided just what you want and are ready to pay you say, *"Compro estas cosas" (KOHM-pro ES-tahs KO-sahs)* (I'm buying these things). If you only want one item, use *esto* if it is masculine or *esta* if it is feminine. If you are buying *un saco (oon SAH-ko)* (a sport coat) you say, *"Compro esto" (KOHM-pro ES-to)* (I'm buying this). Or, if you are buying *una corbata (OO-nah kor-BAH-tah)* (a necktie), *"Compro esta" (KOHM-pro ES-tah)* (I'm buying this). Or, as one store advertises, *¡Me lo llevo! (may lo YAY-vo)* (I'll take it!).

The Colors: *Los Colores*

white	*blanco*
black	*negro*
brown	*café*
gray	*gris*
red	*rojo*
blue	*azul*
yellow	*amarillo*
pink	*rosa*
orange	*naranja*
green	*verde*
maroon	*guinda*
purple	*purpureo, morado*

Chapter 22

Damaged Clothing ... La Ropa Dañada

In the last chapter we looked at *la ropa (la RO-pa)* (clothing) when you are *comprando (kohm-PRAHN-doh)* (buying). Now let's look at how to describe *la ropa dañada (la RO-pa dahn-YAH-dah)* (damaged clothing). If it's new *ropa* you may want to *regresarla (ray-gray-SAR-la)* (return it—the object is tacked on to the infinitive and becomes part of the same word). Or, you may prefer to take it to *un sastre (oon SAH-stray)* (a tailor) or to *una costurera (OO-na ko-stoo-RAY-rah)* (a seamstress) to *reparar (ray-pa-RAR)* (to repair). Both *un sastre* and *una costurera* can *coser (ko-SAIR)* (sew).

With *una falda (OO-nah FALL-dah)* (a skirt) the problem may be simple: *la bastilla (la bah-STEE-yah)* (the hem) *está descosida (es-TAH days-ko-SEE-dah)* (is ripped, or literally unsewn). You can use *descosida* to describe any *costura (ko-STOO-rah)* (seam) that is ripped. For example, *la costura de los pantalones está descosida (la ko-STOO-rah day los pahn-tah-LO-nays es-TAH days-ko-SEE-dah)* (The seam of the pants is ripped—*descosida*, an adjective, ends with an "a" because it modifies *la costura*). *El forro (el FOR-ro)* (the lining) *del abrigo (del ah-BREE-go)* (of the overcoat) *está descosido* (this time *descosido* ends with an "o" because it modifies the masculine *forro*).

If you want to say that something is torn rather than ripped, the word is *roto (RO-toh)* or *rota (RO-tah)*, depending on what it modifies. *El cuello (el KWAY-yo)* (the collar) *del saco (del SAH-ko)* (of the sport coat) *está roto (es-TAH RO-toh)* (is torn). *La espalda (la es-PALL-dah)* (the back) *de la playera (day la ply-AY-rah)* (of the tee-shirt) *está rota.* This may be a problem for *el sastre,* or it may just be *de moda (day MO-dah)* (fashionable). *La manga (la MAHN-gah)* (the sleeve) *de la blusa (day la BLOO-sah)* (of the blouse) *está rota. Roto* also means "broken" when referring to hard items, such as *el vaso (el VAH-so)* (the glass) *está roto (is broken).* Thus, it can also be used to describe a broken zipper: *el cierre (el see-AIR-ray) de la bota (day la BO-tah)* (of the boot) *está roto. Cierre* literally translates as "closer" and in the border area you will also hear *"ziper" (SEE-pair)* (zipper, borrowed from the English and "Mexicanized").

If you want to point out that something is worn, then you use the word *gastado (gah-STAH-doh)* (worn or literally spent). *El puño (el POON-yo)* (the cuff of the sleeve) *de la camisa (day la kah-MEE-sah)* (of the shirt) *está gastado (es-TAH gah-STAH-doh)* (is worn). *El cuello de la blusa está gastado* (the collar of the blouse is worn). Here again, you end the word with an "a" if it modifies a feminine noun: **una bastilla gastada** (a worn hem).

If you have lost a little weight, you will want to have **el sastre hacer más chica** *(ah-SAIR mas CHEE-kah)* (make smaller) **la ropa.** Or, if you have gained weight, **la costurera** can **hacer más grande** *(ah-SAIR mas GRAHN-day)* (make bigger) **la ropa.** Well, a little, at least.

Whether you visit Mexico's **sastres** and **costureras** to **reparar la ropa dañada, arreglar** *(ar-ray-GLAR)* (fix) **la ropa que no le queda,** or to **mandar hacer** *(mahn-DAR ah-SAIR)* (to order to have made) **un traje** *(oon TRAH-hay)* (a suit) or **un vestido** *(oon vay-STEE-doh)* (a dress), you will find them to be a bargain. And with **la ropa dañada** remember: **una puntada** *(OO-nah poon-TAH-dah)* (a stitch) **a tiempo** *(ah tee-EM-po)* (in time) **evita nueve** *(ay-VEE-tah noo-WAY-vay)* (saves or avoids nine, from the verb **evitar**).

It takes time and practice to learn a language. It can't be done en **el abrir y cerrar de los ojos** *(en el ah-BREER ee sair-RAR day los OH-hos)* (literally in the opening and closing of the eyes, or in the wink of an eye). Keep practicing, and look at how far you have come!

More Clothing
... Más Ropa

When buying *la ropa (la RO-pa)* (clothing) you may have the trying experience of trying on an item and then endeavoring to communicate to the Spanish-speaking clerk why it is not *bien (bee-EN)* (okay). This chapter will help you explain to the *empleado (em-play-AH-doh)* (clerk) the exact reason that the clothing *no le queda (no lay KAY-dah)* (doesn't fit you).

When you enter a store, be sure to greet the *empleado* before you start looking around. It is considered extremely impolite in Latin America not to say *"Hola"* when you enter a room, even if you don't know anyone present. *"Buenos Días" (BWAY-nos DEE-ahs)* (good morning) or *"Buenas tardes" (BWAY-nahs TAR-days)* (good afternoon) are never out of place to get the *empleado's* attention and to start things off on a cordial note. He will likely respond, *"¿En qué le puedo servir?" (en kay lay PWAY-doh sair-VEER)* (how may I help you?). Or, *una empleada (OO-nah em-play-AH-dah)* (a saleslady) may approach you when you enter, with the same question. You tell her, *"Busco una blusa" (BOOS-ko OO-nah BLOO-sah)* (I'm looking for a blouse). She'll be happy to show you racks of *blusas* in all sizes and colors. So you take one to the *probador (pru-buh-DOR)* (dressing room).

When you emerge you might want to tell *la empleada* that *"Esta camisa es muy grande" (ES-tah kah-MEE-sah es MOO-ee GRAHN-day)* (this shirt is too large, or very large). If you took a dress to the *probador* you might say, *"Este vestido es muy grande" (ES-tay vay-STEE-doh es MOO-ee GRAHN-day)* (this dress is too large). Note that *esta* is used with feminine nouns and *este* with masculine nouns. While *grande* does not change to reflect gender, *pequeño (pay-KAYN-yo)* (small) does: *Esta blusa es muy pequeña (ES-tah BLOO-sah es MOO-ee pay-KAYN-yah)* (this blouse is too small); *este suéter es muy pequeño (ES-tay SWAY-tair es MOO-ee pay-KAYN-yo)* (this sweater is too small). Most other adjectives also reflect gender (of the item, **not** who wears it) and go after the noun modified. *Este saco es muy largo (ES-tay SAH-ko es MOO-ee LAR-go)* (this blazer or sport coat is too long—**not** large); *esta chamarra es muy larga (ES-tah cha-MAR-rah es MOO-ee LAR-gah)* (this jacket is too long). While many *prendas (PREN-dahs)* (articles of clothing) are singular, some are spoken of in the plural: *Estas pijamas son muy cortas (ES-tahs pee-HA-mas sohn MOO-ee KOR-tahs)* (these pajamas are too short); *estos pantalones son muy cortos (ES-tohs pahn-tah-LO-nays sohn MOO-ee KOR-tohs)* (these pants are too short). Usually, if it is referred to in *inglés* in the plural, it will also be plural in *español*.

The verb and adjective must be changed to reflect the plural, too. *Estos calcetines son muy apretados (ES-tohs kal-say-TEE-nays sohn MOO-ee ah-pray-TAH-dos)* (these socks are too tight); *estas pantuflas son muy apretadas (ES-tas pahn-TOO-flas sohn MOO-ee ah-pray-TAH-dahs)* (these slippers are too tight). Or even, *estos zapatos son muy flojos (ES-tos sah-PA-tos sohn MOO-ee FLO-hos)* (these shoes are too loose).

The word *demasiado (day-ma-see-AH-doh)* may be used to indicate "too much" in place of *muy* which is frequently translated "very." However, *muy* is more common, and is easier to say. *Demasiado* may be used for emphasis: *esta corbata es demasiada fea (ES-ta kor-BAH-ta es day-ma-see-AH-dah FAY-ah)* (this tie is 'way too ugly). *El color de esta sudadera es demasiado feo (el ko-LOR day ES-tah soo-dah-DAY-rah es day-ma-see-AH-doh FAY-oh)* (the color of this sweatshirt is really very ugly)— here *feo* is masculine because it modifies *el color* of *la sudadera,* not *la sudadera* itself. Or, you might say, *"Este color es muy llamativo" (ES-tay ko-LOR es MOO-ee yah-ma-TEE-vo)* (this color is too loud).

Remember, "o" endings usually go with singular masculine *prendas,* "a" endings go with singular feminine *prendas,* "os" goes with plural masculine, and "as" with plural feminine. In *español* adjectives of nouns must agree in gender and number. Practice these expressions. And remember, if *el zapato no le queda* you can always exchange it!

Chapter 24

Housing...
Vivienda

If you are an ***aficionado*** *(ah-fee-see-oh-NAH-doh)* (fan) of Latin America, and don't already have ***una vivienda*** *(OO-nah vee-vee-EN-dah)* (housing), maybe you are thinking about looking for ***una casa*** *(OO-nah KAH-sah)* (a house) or ***un departamento*** *(oon day-par-tah-MEN-toh)* (an apartment) to rent. Keep an eye open for ***letreros*** *(leh-TRAY-ros)* (signs) that say, ***"se renta"*** *(say REN-tah)* (for rent). Then, don't hesitate to ask ***el propietario*** *(el PRO-pee-ay-TAH-ree-oh)* (the landlord) or ***la propietaria*** *(la PRO-pee-ay-TAH-ree-ah)* (the landlady) to show you around ***el domicilio*** *(el doh-mee-SEE-lee-oh)* (the dwelling, the place).

If ***el dueño*** *(el DWAYN-yo)* (the owner—end it in "a" if it's a woman) says that ***el departamento*** has ***dos cuartos*** *(dohs KWAHR-tos)* (two rooms), he probably does not mean ***dos recámaras*** *(dohs ray-KAH-ma-rahs)* (two bedrooms). Many Mexican ***apartamentos*** *(ah-par-tah-MEN-tos)* (apartments, interchangeable with ***departamen-***

tos) are similar to U.S. efficiency apartments or studios. These are usually *barato (bah-RAH-toh)* (cheap) and adequate if you are not too *exigente (ek-see-HEN-tay)* (fussy, particular). But for a family, *es muy pequeño (es MOO-ee peh-KAYN-yo)* (it's very small).

If you have *una familia (OO-nah fah-MEE-lee-ah)* (a family) *grande (GRAHN-day)* (big—adjectives go after the word they modify), you will want something *más grande* (bigger). Perhaps *el dueño* can *enseñarle (en-sen-YAR-lay)* (show you, the same verb means to teach) *una casa ámplia (AHM-plee-ah)* (another word for large, ample).

Coming through *la puerta principal (la PWAYR-tah preen-see-PALL)* (the front or main door) he will show you *la sala (la SAH-la)* (the living room) and, perhaps *el comedor (el ko-may-DOR)* (the dining room). *A la derecha (ah la day-RAY-cha)* (on the right) might be *la cocina (la ko-SEE-nah)* (the kitchen) and *el cuarto de lavar (el KWAHR-toh day la-VAR)* (the laundry room). *A la izquierda (ah la ees-kee-AIR-dah)* (on the left) could be *el pasillo (el pa-SEE-yoh)* (the hallway) which goes to *las recámaras* and *el baño (el BAHN-yo)* (the bathroom). *Afuera (ah-FWAY-rah)* (outside) will be *la cochera (la ko-CHAY-rah)* or *el garage (el gah-RAH-hay)* (two words for garage).

You will want to ask *el propietario, "¿Está amueblado?" (es-TAH ahm-WAY-blah-doh)* (is it furnished?). Or, is it *sin mobiliario (seen mo-bee-lee-AH-ree-oh)* (unfurnished, literally without furnishings). Other good questions: *¿Incluye agua? (een-KLOO-yay AH-gwah)* (is water included?); *¿Incluye luz? (een-KLOO-yay loos)* (are lights or electricity included?). *El dueño* may reply, *"Incluye agua* (water is included), *el inquilino (el een-kee-LEE-no)* (the tenant) *paga la luz (PA-gah la loos)* (pays the lights).

Any *reparaciones (ray-pa-rah-see-OH-nays)* (repairs) should be completed before you move in. Once you take possession, there is no guarantee that anything will get *arreglado (ar-ray-GLAH-doh)* (fixed). And anything *descompuesto (des-kohm-PWAY-sto)* (broken, not working) is pretty much the responsibility of *el inquilino.* Customs and laws are different in Mexico, but it's a wonderful place to *vivir (vee-VEER)* (to live) and to *visitar (vee-see-TAR)* (to visit). Be sure to check with a lawyer if this is your first adventure in renting in Mexico.

Rentar (ren-TAR) (renting) *una casa* or *un departamento* is a good way to decide if you want to *comprar (kohm-PRAR)* (to buy). And it means that you won't be *formándose (for-MAHN-doh-say)* (standing in line) to check into a hotel—or to be told "no vacancy." Your little piece of *paraiso (pa-ry-EE-so)* (paradise) will be *garantizado (gah-rahn-tee-SAH-doh)* (guaranteed) for the length of your *contrato (kohn-TRAH-toh)* (lease, contract). And just think what a lot of practice you will get with your *español!*

Chapter 25

Housework ...
Aseo de Casa

If you are one of the lucky ones who finds that living in Mexico, or near it, allows you the luxury of having *una sirvienta (OO-nah seer-vee-EN-tah)* (a maid) you may need some *español (es-pahn-YOL)* (Spanish) to be able to talk to her. Or perhaps you just have *una señora que ayuda con la limpieza (OO-nah sen-YO-rah kay i-YOO-da kohn la leem-pee-AY-sah)* (a cleaning lady, literally a lady who helps with the cleaning) who comes in *cada semana (KAH-dah say-MA-nah)* (each week). You need to tell her what you want her to do. With this chapter we will do away with the wild gesticulations. You will be able to direct *el aseo de la casa (el ah-SAY-oh day la KAH-sah)* (the housework) in a civilized manner.

En la cocina (en la ko-SEE-nah) (in the kitchen) you may want to tell her to *lavar los platos (la-VAR los PLAH-tos)* (wash the dishes). *"Favor de lavar los platos"* is the easy way to make a request or polite command. By saying, *"Favor de . . ."* *(fah-VOR day)* (please), the need to conjugate the verb is eliminated. Just fill in the space with the verb infinitive (that's the form of the verb that the dictionary gives). Give her *la escoba (la es-KO-bah)* (the broom) and let her *barrer (bar-RAIR)* (sweep) *el piso (el PEE-so)* (the floor). Afterward, she can *trapear (trah pay AR)* (mop) and *encerar (en-say-RAR)* (wax) it.

En la sala (en la SAH-lah) (in the living room) she will need *un trapo (oon TRAH-po)* (a rag) so that she can *sacudir (sah-koo-DEER)* (dust) *los muebles (los MWAY-blays)* (the furniture). If you have *una alfombra (OO-nah all-FOAM-bra)* (a carpet) you will want her to *limpiar (leem-pee-AR)* (clean) *con la aspiradora (kohn la ah-spee-rah-DOH-rah)* (with the vacuum cleaner).

En la recámara (en la ray-KAH-ma-rah) (in the bedroom) she can *cambiar las sábanas (kahm-bee-AR las SAH-bah-nahs)* (change the sheets) *de la cama (day la KAH-mah)* (on the bed). If you have asked her to *lavar la ropa (la-VAR la RO-pa)* (wash the clothes), when she finishes she can *acomodar la ropa (ah-ko-mo-DAR la RO-pa)* (put away the clothes).

Moving on to *el baño (el BAHN-yo)* (the bathroom), she can *fregar (fray-GAR)* (scour) *el lavamanos (el la-va-MA-nos)* (the basin), *la tina (la TEE-nah)* (the bathtub), and *la taza (la TAH-sah)* (the toilet). If you have a shower instead of a *tina*, in America it is known as *una regadera (OO-nah ray-gah-DAY-rah)* rather than the European *ducha (DOO-cha)*.

Ask her to *regar las plantas (ray-GAR las PLAHN-tahs)* (water the plants) *en el patio (en el PA-tee-oh)* (in the patio or yard) and *limpiar los cristales de las ventanas (leem-pee-AR los kree-STAH-lays day las ven-TAH-nahs)* (clean the glass of the windows) *por toda la casa (por TOH-dah la KAH-sah)* (throughout the house).

With all this work, don't forget to give her *un descanso (oon des-KAHN-so)* (a rest) now and then. At *mediodía (MEH-dee-oh-DEE-ah)* (noon or midday) give her *la comida (la ko-MEE-dah)* (lunch). But most of all, when she goes home, tell her, *"Muchas gracias por un trabajo bien hecho,"* *(MOO-chas GRAH-see-ahs por oon trah-BAH-ho bee-EN AY-cho)* (thanks a lot for a job well done).

Even if you don't have *una sirvienta* you can still practice these words by talking to yourself while you do *el aseo de la casa.* Then you'll be ready when you *saca la lotería (SAH-kah la lo-tay-REE-ah)* (win the lottery). As you work around the house, you can say to yourself, *"Voy a lavar los trastes,"* *(voy ah la-VAR los TRAH-stays)* (I'm going to wash the dishes—*trastes* is a synonym for *platos*). Using *"Voya_____"* (I'm going to _____) is another way to use the verb in its infinitive form, without having to conjugate it.

Voy a sacudir la mesa (la MAY-sah) (the table), is a good way to practice your new language and get *el aseo de la casa* done at the same time. Practice making up new combinations of these words and phrases. For instance, *Voy a limpiar la cocina* (I'm going to clean the kitchen); *voy a barrer el patio* (I'm going to sweep the patio). You will be surprised at how many things you can say by changing a few words around.

And, *por supuesto (por soo-PWAY-sto)* (of course), if you do have *una señora que ayuda con la limpieza,* she will marvel at your new ability to communicate with her intelligently. She may even *lavar* and *fregar* with more energy, so that your house will sparkle.

Chapter 26

Home Repair: Reparar La Casa

How are things *alrededor de (all-ray-day-DOR day)* (around) the old *hacienda (ah-see-EN-dah)* (homestead)? Do you have *un poco de trabajo (oon PO-ko day trah-BAH-ho)* (a little work) that needs to be done on *la casa (la KAH-sah)* (the house)? Maybe something *está roto (es-TAH RO-toh)* (is broken). *Tal vez (tall vays)* (perhaps) you want to *remodelar (ray-mo-day-LAR)* (remodel) your home, or add on *un cuarto (oon KWAHR-toh)* (a room).

This is the chapter that will teach you how to talk to *los trabajadores (los trah-bah-ha-DOH-rays)* (the workmen) in *español*.

If *la coladera (la ko-la-DAY-rah)* (the drain) in *el lavabo (el la-VAH-bo)* (the basin) *está tapada (es-TAH tah-PA-dah)* (is stopped up) then you need *un plomero (oon ploh-MAY-ro)* (a plumber). He will *destapar (des-tah-PAR)* (unclog) it. He also can *ayudar (I-oo-DAR)* (help) if *el excusado (el ex-koo-SAH-doh)* (the toilet) *no traga (no TRAH-gah)* (won't flush). Or, if *la llave (la YAH-vay)* (the faucet—the same word as for key or wrench) *está goteando (es-TAH go-tay-AHN-doh)* (is dripping), *el plomero* will *reparar (ray-pa-RAR)* (repair) it with his *llave* (wrench). Your *calentón de agua (kah-len-TOHN day AH-gwah)* (water heater) *no funciona (no foon-see-ON-nah)* (doesn't work)? Once again, *el plomero* to the rescue.

Thinking of putting in *un ventilador (oon ven-tee-la-DOR)* (a fan) *en el cielo (en el see-AY-lo)* (in the ceiling—yes, it also means sky)? Call *un electricista (oon eh-layk-tree-SEES-tah)* (an electrician). He can also *instalar (een-stah-LAR)* (install) *un contacto (oon kohn-TAHK-toh)* (an outlet), even *un contacto con tierra (kohn tee-AY-rah)* (a grounded outlet) if necessary. If you need *un circuito (oon seer-KOO-ee-toh)* (a circuit) of *doscientos veinte (doh-see-EN-tos BAYN-tay)* (220) instead of *ciento diez (see-EN-toh dee-ES)* (110), *el electricista* is your man. When you need to *instalar una luz (OO-nah loos)* (to install a light), fix *los alambres (los ah-LAHM-brays)* (the wiring) or put in *un timbre (oon TEEM-bray)* (a bell), *el electricista* can *arreglar (ah-ray-GLAR)* (fix) it.

Want to *construir (kohn-stroo-EER)* (build) *un cuarto*? Or maybe add *una ropera (OO-nah ro-PAY-rah)* (a closet) in *la recámara (la ray-KAH-ma-rah)* (the bedroom)? Better get *un carpintero (oon kar-peen-TAY-ro)* (a carpenter). He can build *un techo (oon TAY-cho)* (a roof) for your *patio* or *instalar una puerta corridiza (OO-nah PWAYR-tah kor-ree-DEE-sah)* (a sliding door). Want some *entrepaños (en-tray-PAHN-yos)* (built-in shelves)? *El carpintero* is the one to call.

El carpintero de techo (the roofer) will put *brea (BRAY-ah)* (tar) and *papel arenado (pa-PAIL ah-ray-NAH-doh)* (roofing paper) on your *techo* if it needs it. As with everything *hoy día (oy DEE-ah)* (nowdays), *los traba-jadores* specialize. A roofer is a *carpintero de obra negra (day OH-bra NAY-grah)* (a dirty-work carpenter, literally "of black work"). A finish carpenter is a *carpintero de obra blanca (day OH bra BLAIIN-kah)* (a clean work carpenter, literally "of white work").

If you need *rejas (RAY-has)* (bars) for your *ventanas (ven-TAH-nahs)* (windows), you look for *un herrero (oon air-RAY-ro)* (an iron worker). He can *soldar (sol-DAR)* (weld) anything, including *tubería (too-bay-REE-ah)* (pipes), *puertas* (gates) and *escaleras de hierro (es-kah-LAY-rahs day YAY-roh)* (iron stairways).

Finally, when you're ready to *pintar (peen-TAR)* (to paint), get *un pintor (oon peen-TOR)* (a painter). If you are using *un color claro (oon ko-LOR KLAH-ro)* (a light color), you may want him to put on *dos manos (dohs MA-nos)* (two coats—the same word means "hands" also). If your color is *más obscuro (mas ohb-SKOO-ro)* (darker) you probably only need *una mano* or *una capa (OO-nah KAH-pa)* (one coat). *El pintor* may work with *un rodillo (oon ro-DEE-yo)* (a roller) or with *una brocha (OO-nah BRO-cha)* (a brush). And be sure that he has plenty of *thinner (TEE-nair)* (thinner) to clean up.

When talking to *trabajadores,* a picture is worth a thousand words. Sketch on paper or draw in the dirt with a stick so that you can both have a good idea exactly what you want done. Remember that whatever small crises may happen around *la casa,* there is a *trabajador* who specializes in *arreglar* these things.

Chapter 27

Driving: Manejar

In the border areas of Mexico you can usually get along pretty well with *poco (PO-ko)* (little) or no *español*. In *el restaurante (el rest-ow-RAHN-tay)* (the restaurant), you can point at what you want on *el menú (el may-NOO)* (the menu). In *la tienda (la tee-EN-dah)* (the store) they can usually tell you *el precio (el PRAY-see-oh)* (the price) in *inglés* or write it down. But if you drive, you need to know what *las señales (las sen-YAH-lays)* (the signs) mean. They can warn you of *peligro (pay-LEE-gro)* (danger), tell you when there is a *camino cerrado (ka-MEE-no sair-RAH-doh)* (road closed) or when you must *ceda el paso (SAY-dah el PA-so)* (yield), and other life-saving information.

Fortunately the *alto (ALL-toh)* or *pare (PAH-ray)* (stop) sign and *el semáforo (el seh-MA-fo-ro)* (the traffic light) are the same colors as their U.S. counterparts. Remember that *la velocidad máxima (la vay-lo-see-DAHD MAHK-see-ma)* (the maximum speed, or speed limit) is given in kilometers per hour, not miles. Where they are really serious about the *velocidad máxima*, they install *topes (TOH-pays)* (speed bumps).

When you see *no rebasar (no ray-bah-SAR)* (no passing) you'll have to stay behind that *camión (kah-mee-OHN)* (truck) that is going so *despacio (des-PA-see-oh)* (slow). And be sure to watch out for *peatones (pay-ah-TOH-nays)* (pedestrians).

There are numerous *señales* the length of Baja's Highway 1 that advise of a *vado (VAH-doh)*. This is usually translated "dip," but really means a ford: a place to cross through a river without a bridge. In the desert this can be important to remember. While the *vados* are usually dry, during and after a heavy rain they will suddenly become rivers, some of which are very *peligrosos (pay-lee-GRO-sos)* (dangerous) to cross.

Back in the city *circulación (seer-koo-la-see-OHN)* with an arrow will tell you to keep right or left. Or, the *señal* may say *conserve su derecha (kohn-SAIR-vay soo day-RAY-cha)* (keep right) or *conserve su izquierda (ees-kee-AIR-dah)* (left). *Doble circulación (DOH-blay seer-koo-la-see-OHN)* (two-way traffic) is pretty easy to deal with, but keep an eye out for *calles (KY-ays)* (streets) that are *un solo sentido (oon SO-lo sen-TEE-doh)* (one way), or possibly just marked *solo (SO-lo)* (only) with an arrow.

Desviación (des-vee-ah-see-OHN) (detour) frequently means that there are *hombres trabajando (OHM-brays trah-bah-HAHN-doh)* (men working). Often there is *peligro (pay-LEE-gro)* (danger) and one must *manejar (ma-nay-HAR)* (drive) with *cuidado (kwee-DAH-doh)* (care) or *precaución (pray-cow-see-OWN)* (caution). A *desviación* and a *curva peligrosa (KOOR-vah pay-lee-GRO-sah)* (dangerous curve) are both good reasons to go *despacio.*

Two frequently ignored signs are found on the *cuota (koo-OH-tah)* (toll) road: *Carril izquierdo solo para rebasar (kah-REEL ees-kee-AIR-doh SO-lo PA-rah ray-bah-SAR)* (left lane for passing only)—that guy dawdling along in the inside *carril* obviously hasn't heard about life in the fast lane. And, **no tire basura** *(no TEE-ray bah-SOO-rah)* (don't litter, or literally, don't throw trash) has nothing to do with the **llantas** *(YAHN-tahs)* (tires) of your **carro** *(KAR-ro)* (car).

As luck would have it, the Mexican government had the foresight to put up lots of signs for people who are not literate in any language. These have pictures that can usually be deciphered, or at least serve as neutral symbols for fantasies. They indicate **zona de derrumbes** *(SO-nah day dair-ROOM-bays)* (landslide zone or falling rocks), **sanitarios** *(sah-nee-TAR-ee-ohs)* (rest rooms) and a host of other roadside attractions. So, as you go down the **carretera** *(kar-ray-TAY-rah)* (highway), I hope that you have **semáforos verdes y no peligro.**

Chapter 28

Mechanic . . .
El Mecánico

When you are **viajando** *(vee-ah-HAHN-doh)* (traveling) in Latin America there is no need to worry if your **carro** *(KAR-ro)* (car) **falla** *(FY-yah)* (breaks down, fails). There are plenty of **mecánicos** *(may-KAH-nee-kos)* (mechanics) and **talleres** *(ty-YAIR-rays)* (repair garages).

As in the States, some are specialists. If your **claxón** *(klak-SOHN)* (horn) **no pita** *(no PEE-tah)* (doesn't honk), you'll need a **taller eléctrico** *(ty-YAIR eh-LAYK-tree-ko)* (auto electric shop). If your **silenciador** *(see-len-see-ah-DOR)* (muffler) is too loud, go to a **taller** that specializes in **mofles y soldadura** *(MO-flays ee sol-dah-DOO-rah)* (mufflers and soldering). **Mofle** is a little more common in the border area than **silenciador**, but is a "Spanglish" word.

If **la defensa** *(la day-FEN-sah)* (the bumper) and **el guardafango** *(el gwar-dah-FAHN-go)* (the fender) are crumpled, you'll need a **carrocería** *(kar-ro-say-REE-ah)* (body shop). And if *los frenos (los FRAY-nos)* (the brakes) *no funcionan (no foon-see-OH-nan)* (don't work, don't function) get them fixed *de una vez (day OO-nah vays)* (at once).

Many of the words that deal with *los carros* are borrowed from English. This is because *las partes (las PAR-tays)* (the parts) are frequently obtained in the U.S. So with very little *español*, you can make yourself understood at the *taller*. And you'll pay less than in the States.

When you are at the *taller, el mecánico* may ask you to *arrancar (ar-rahn-KAR)* (to start) *el auto (el OW-toh)* (the car). Or, he may say, *"Echele a andar" (AY-cheh-lay ah ahn-DAR)*, another way of saying to start *el motor (el mo-TOR)* (the motor). When he wants you to turn it off, he'll say, *"Apáguelo" (ah-PA-gay-lo)* (turn it off).

If you leave the car at the *taller, el mecánico* will need *la llave (la YAH-vay)* (the key). You can *regresar (ray-gray-SAR)* (return) *más tarde (mas TAR-day)* (later, literally "more later"). Be sure to get *un presupuesto (oon pray-soo-PWAY-sto)* (an estimate) so that you'll have an idea of the cost. There is no law in Latin America that prevents the *mecánico* from going more than ten percent over the estimate when he gives you the final bill. But if he exceeds *el presupuesto* too much, *quejarse (kay-HAR-say)* (complaining) may get him to lower *la cuenta (la KWAYN-tah)* a little.

When *los faros (los FAH-ros)* (the headlights) don't work, *el mecánico* will first check *los fusibles (los foo-SEE-blays)* (the fuses). This is fairly easy and cheaper than replacing *el foco (el FO-ko)* (the light bulb). It is important that all of *las luces (las LOO-says)* (the lights) on a car *funcionan*.

Cuando menos esperado (KWAHN-doh MAY-nos es-pay-RAH-doh) (when least expected), you can *ponchar (pon-CHAR)* (puncture) *una llanta (OO-nah YAHN-tah)* (a tire). Hopefully you carry *una extra (OO-nah EHK-strah)* (a spare) and *un gato (oon GAH-toh)* (a jack—yes, it means "cat" too) *en la cajuela (en la kah-WHAY-la)* (in the trunk). Later you can *arreglar (ar-ray-GLAR)* (fix) *la llanta ponchada (pohn-CHA-dah)* (punctured or flat tire).

It's important to *cambiar el aceite (kahm-bee-AR el ah-SAY-tay)* (to change the oil) and *poner a punto (po-NAIR ah POON-toh)* (tune up) your auto periodically. You will also hear the expression *tunap (TOO-nop)* (tune up) in *la frontera.* This will keep your *carro* running right.

When you're sitting at *el volante (el vo-LAHN-tay)* (the steering wheel) and *el motor* is purring, you'll feel great. May you drive with *cuidado* under *cielos (see-AY-los)* (skies) *azules (ah-SOO-lays)* (blue) when you *manejar (ma-nay-HAR)* (drive).

Chapter 29

Directions ...

Instrucciones

Some people have difficulty finding their way around south of the border. If you have a tendency to *perderse (pair-DAIR-say)* (to get yourself lost) or if you have trouble finding your way around *el bárrio (el BAR-ree-oh)* (the Latin quarter, neighborhood), this chapter has some phrases that will help.

To ask where something is you say: *"¿Dónde está _____?" (DOHN-day es-TAH)*. You can fill in the blank with words like *el cine (el SEE-nay)* (the movie theater), *el banco (el BAHN-ko)* (the bank), *el aeropuerto (el I-ro-PWAYR-toh)* (the airport), or *el Palácio Municipal (el pah-LA-see-oh moo-nee-se-PAHL)* (City Hall). For example, *¿Dónde está el correo? (DOHN-day es-TAH el kor-RAY-oh)* (Where is the post office?) or *¿Dónde está el parque? (DOHN-day es-TAH el PAR-kay)* (Where is the park?).

Of course, **entender** *(en-ten-DAIR)* (to understand) the answer to your question is another problem. If you are **cerca de** *(SAIR-kah day)* (close to) the place, some responses might be **allá** *(i-YAH)* (over there), **en frente** *(en FREN-tay)* (across the street—I know it sounds like "in front" but cross the street anyway), **en la esquina** *(on la es-KEE-nah)* (on the corner), or **dando vuelta a la esquina** *(DAHN-doh VWAYL-tah a la es-KEE-nah)* (around the corner). Practice these expressions out loud to become familiar with them.

If you are **lejos de** *(LAY-hos day)* (far from) the place you ask about, be prepared for lots of **instrucciones** *(een-strook-see-OH-nays)* (directions). If you don't catch them all, begin going in the direction indicated and stop and ask again when you are **más cerca** (closer, or literally "more close"). Remember, some people speak more distinctly than others, and their **español** is easier to understand.

If you ask **"¿Dónde está el terminal de autobuses?** *(DOHN-day es-TAH el tair-mee-NAHL day OW-toh-BOO-says)* (where is the bus station?) you may hear, **"Está a diez cuadras al este de aquí"** *(es-TAH ah dee-ES KWAH-drahs all ES-tay day ah-KEE)* (It's ten blocks to the east of here). A few people use the word **manzanas** *(mahn-SAH-nahs)* for blocks; they aren't talking about apples.

The points of the **brújula** *(BROO-hoo-la)* (compass) are **el norte** *(el NOR-tay)* (north), **el sur** *(el soor)* (south), **el este** *(el ES-tay)* (east) and **el oeste** *(el oh-WES-tay)* (west). So, if you ask, **"¿Dónde está el hospital?"** *(DOHN-day es-TAH el ohs-pee-TALL)* (Where is the hospital?), the reply may be **"Vaya al norte dos millas y de vuelta hacia el oeste"** *(VI-yah all NOR-tay dohs MEE-yahs ee day VWAYL-tah AH-see-ah el oh-WES-tay)* (go north two miles and turn toward the west). When speaking about **caminos** *(kah-MEE-nos)* (roads, highways), you'll sometimes hear **oriente** *(oh-ree-EN-tay)* for east and **poniente** *(po-nee-EN-tay)* for west.

Dar vuelta *(dar VWAYL-tah)* (literally, "to give a turn") means to turn. You just conjugate *dar* (to give) for the correct person and add *vuelta*. In the present tense it goes like this:

doy vuelta	I turn
das vuelta	you turn (familiar)
da vuelta	you turn, he or she turns
damos vuelta	we turn
dan vuelta	you all turn or they turn

You can use it to say *Doy vuelta a la izquierda (doy VWAYL-tah ah la ees-kee-AIR-dah)* (I turn to the left), or *dan vuelta a la derecha (dahn VWAYL-tah ah la day-RAY-cha)* (you all turn right).

Be careful of word endings in Spanish—they make a lot of difference! *Derecho (day-RAY-cho)*, ending in "o" means straight ahead, and *derecha*, ending in "a" means to the right. So if someone tells you *Vaya derecho* (go straight ahead), DON'T turn right!

As you go searching *a la derecha y a la izquierda*, asking *instrucciones* and getting *más cerca*, someone will eventually say, "*Está aquí" (es-TAH ah-KEE)* (it is here). You will have arrived. And you will have had an adventure in *español* along the way.

Chapter 30

Getting Lost
... Perderse

One day in Ensenada, I had a very funny *plática (PLAH-tee-ka)* (discussion, chat) which rivaled Abbott and Costello's famous "Who's on First?" for humor. I stopped by **una cenaduría** *(OO-nah say-nah-doo-REE-ah)* (a diner) for a bowl of **caldo** *(KAL-doh)* (soup) and asked the **mesera** *(meh-SAY-rah)* (waitress) for directions to a certain **colónia** *(ko-LO-nee-ah)* (neighborhood). She told me to **dar vuelta** *(dar VWAYL-tah)* on Lopez Mateos Av. and go to *Av. Reforma.*

"**Da vuelta a la derecha**," *(dah VWAYL-tah ah la day-RAY-cha)* (you turn right), she said. Then, continue "**hasta** *(AH-stah)* (until) **la plaza comercial** *(la PLAH-sah ko-mair-see-ALL)* (the shopping center). From there, **va por Delante**" *(vah por day-LAHN-tay)* (you go forward).

Realizing that going forward would take me to the town of Maneadero, but not to the *colónia* I sought, I asked, *"¿Doy vuelta a la derecha?"* (do I turn right?).

"No, vaya por Delante," she affirmed.

"¿Sigo hacia el sur?" *(SEE-go AH-see-ah el soor)* (do I continue south?), I inquired.

"No, va por Delante."

"¿Doy vuelta a la izquierda?" *(doy VWAYL-tah ah la ees-kee-AIR-dah)* (do I turn left?).

"No, derecho por Delante" *(no day-RAY-cho por day-LAHN-tay)* (no, straight ahead forward).

We repeated this two or three times, hoping for clarification. Certainly, I thought, I wouldn't go *para atrás (PA-rah ah-TROS)* (backward). Realizing that things would not become any clearer and fearing that she thought I was *muy torpe (MOO-ee TOR-pay)* (very dense, dull-witted), I thanked her and paid for the *caldo.* I knew from experience that Mexican directions are not always *claro (KLAH-ro)* (clear; it also means "of course"). You can follow them as far as you understand, then ask someone else.

Reaching the intersection of the *plaza comercial,* I knew that the *dirección (dee-rayk-see-OHN)* (address) I was seeking must be *para arriba (PA-rah ah-REE-bah)* (toward the hills and away from the ocean, literally "up"), so I turned *a la izquierda.* I had driven several *cuadras (KWAH-drahs)* (blocks) before I found a street sign and realized that I was on *Avenida Delante (ah-vay-NEE-dah day-LAHN-tay) (Delante* or Forward Avenue). *Las instrucciones (las een-strook-see-OH-nays)* (the directions) the *mesera* had given me became clear! She had told me to go *por Delante,* meaning *Av. Delante.* I had not heard the capital "D" and presumed that she meant forward.

Adelante (ah-day-LAHN-tay) also means "forward" and is one way to tell people to come in when you answer the door. *Pase usted (PA-say oo-STED)* (come in, singular) and *pasen ustedes (PA-sen oo-STAY-des)* (come in, plural, when speaking to more than one person) are from the verb *pasar (pa-SAR)* (to pass). They are also used to invite someone into your house. However *venir (vay-NEER)* (to come) is not used in this way.

Be careful with words which seem almost the same in both languages—sometimes they are equivalent and sometimes not. For example, *discutir (dees-koo-TEER)* means to argue, not to discuss. If you want to discuss, use *hablar (ah-BLAR)* (to speak) or *platicar (plah-tee-KAR)* (to chat). Directions are *instrucciones* but not *direcciones*, because that is an address or house number.

Asking for *instrucciones* is a wonderful way to practice your Spanish and to explore. The more you do it, the easier it becomes to ask *"¿Dónde está . . .?" (DOHN-day es-TAH)* (where is . . .?). It takes time, study and practice to understand the answer you get. Don't be discouraged if you happen to *perderse (pair-DAIR-say)* (to get lost). Think of it as an adventure! Keep asking *"¿Dónde está . . .?"* of different people. Someone will point you in the right direction. And with each conversation you will be getting closer and closer to your goal.

Chapter 31

Cycling ......
Cyclismo

Recently, a popular bicycling magazine listed the ten biggest rides in California. Strangely enough, the list was preceded by two very popular rides in Baja California, not California, **Estados Unidos** *(es-TAH-dohs oo-NEE-dohs)*. With so many **gringos** cruising the countryside on their **bicicletas** *(bee-see-KLAY-tahs)* (bicycles), let's take a look at some biking **español.**

     The Rosarito-to-Ensenada **viaje** *(vee-AH-hay)* (trip) is not really a **carrera** *(kah-RAY-rah)* (race). It is **cincuenta** *(seen-KWAYN-tah)* (fifty) **millas** *(MEE-yahs)*, or **ochenta** *(oh-CHEN-tah)* (eighty) **kilometros** *(kee-LO-may-tros)* that people ride just **para diversión** *(PA-rah dee-vair-see-OHN)* (for fun). In fact, it is so popular that it is held twice a year—**en abril** *(en ah-BREEL)* (in April) **y en septiembre** *(ee en sep-tee-EM-bray)* (and in September). Each time it draws up to 16,000 participants, or more! The oldest Baja bike ride is the Tecate-Ensenada, **setenta y cinco millas** *(say-TEN-tah ee SEEN-ko MEE-yahs)* (seventy-five miles) of **montañas** *(mohn-TAHN-yahs)* (mountains) leading down to **la orilla del mar** *(la oh-REE-yah del mar)* (the shore of the sea). This one has been ridden for the past **veinte** *(BAY-een-tay)* (twenty) **años** *(AHN-yos)* (years)

Baja is full of beautiful **paisajes** *(py-SAH-hays)* (scenery). You can get some **ejercicio** *(eh-hair-SEE-see-oh)* (exercise) and have fun, even when there is no organized **viaje de bicicletas.** Get together with some friends and get in shape—especially if you are contemplating joining either of the rides mentioned. You will want to **revisar** *(ray-vee-SAR)* (check) your **bici** *(BEE-see)* (short for **bicicleta,** bike). Be sure that **las ruedas** *(las roo-AY-dahs)* (the wheels) move easily and that **las llantas** *(las YAWN-tahs)* (the tires) are properly inflated. Bring your own **medidor** *(may-dee-DOR)* (gauge) to the **gasolinera** *(gah-so-lee-NAY-rah)* (gas station); the usual Mexican method of testing for proper pressure is to pound on the **llanta** with your fist a couple of times—not too accurate. Be sure that **los frenos** *(los FRAY-nos)* (the brakes) work well. You'll need them on those **montañas.** **Los cambios** *(los KAHM-bee-ohs)* (the gears) should shift readily, and **la cadena** *(la kah-DAY-nah)* (the chain) should be lightly oiled. Be sure to **revisar** for **rayos** *(RY-ohs)* (spokes) that might be bent, too.

Once **el asiento** *(el ah-see-EN-toh)* (the seat) is properly adjusted so that your **pies** *(PEE-ays)* (feet) are comfortable on the **pedales** *(peh-DAH-lays)* (pedals), and you have your **casco** *(KAHS-ko)* (helmet) firmly on your **cabeza** *(kah-BAY-sah)* (head) you are ready to take off. You may feel more secure if you have a **claxón** *(klak-SOHN)* or **pito** *(PEE-toh)* (two different words for horn). It will let you warn the cars that you are near if you have to ride in traffic. But there is no substitute for **cuidado** *(kwee-DAH-doh)* (care). **Luces** *(LOO-says)* (lights) and **reflectores** *(ray-flek-TOH-rays)* (reflectors) are more of the safety equipment you will need if you ride after dark—a very dangerous activity, but occasionally necessary. Avoid it at all costs, nevertheless.

Las bicicletas de carrera (racing bikes) have a *chasis (CHA-sees)* (frame) that is lightweight, but largely suited to smooth pavement as is rarely found in Mexico. *Las bicicletas de montaña* (mountain bikes) have a *chasis* that is heavier and will withstand the rough wear that Mexican riding gives them. When you *andar en bicicleta (ahn-DAR en bee-see-KLAY-tah)* (ride a bike) in Baja, you frequently do some off-road riding, even if that is not what you had planned. If you ride in all kinds of *tiempo (tee-EM-po)* (weather), a *guardafangos (gwar-dah-FAHN-gos)* (fender) will help eliminate the stripe up your back when you ride in wet weather.

The laid-back pace in Mexico readily lends itself to biking, *para diversión* or as a means of transportation. It is economical, good *ejercicio,* and efficient. If you have ever been wedged into a rush-hour bus or taxi that made stops at every corner, you know that the wind in your hair as you speed by on a bike is a real plus. And you get to your destination at about the same time as the public transport. At any rate, for an organized *viaje, una carrera,* or transportation, *¡una bicicleta en México es mucha diversión!*

Chapter 32

Haircut ...

Corte De Pelo

Have you ever tried to get your hair cut in Mexico? The service is cheaper than in the U.S. but the results depend on how much **español** you speak. *Un corte de cabello (oon KOR-tay day kah-BAY-yo)* (a haircut) can be obtained in a *salón de belleza (sa-LOHN day bay-YAY-sah)* or *salón estética (sa-LOHN es-TAY-tee-kah)* (two ways to say beauty salon). These generally serve both men and women—**unisex** *(OO-nee-sex)*! Or, if you are a man, you can go to the *peluquería (pay-loo-kay-REE-ah)* (barbershop) *en la esquina (en la es-KEE-nah)* (on the corner). The word *peluquería* comes from *peluca (pay-LOO-kah)* (wig) from the days when everyone, men and women, wore wigs.

Whether your hair is *lácio (LA-see-oh)* (straight), *ondulado (ohn-doo-LA-doh)* (wavy), or *chino (CHEE-no)* (curly), you will have to tell the *estilista (es-tee-LEE-stah)* (stylist) how you want it cut: *parejo (pa-RAY-ho)* (an even, blunt cut) or *en capas (en KA-pas)* (layered). Men can choose *con (kohn)* (with) or *sin (seen)* (without) *patillas (pa-TEE-yahs)* (sideburns). Both sexes can choose *con* or *sin flequito (flay-KEE-toh)* (bangs).

If you have split ends you may want your *pelo (PAY-lo)* (hair) *despuntado (des-poon-TAH-doh)* (trimmed at the ends). Or, if your hair is very thick, you may want to *entresacarlo (en-tray-sah-KAR-lo)* (thin it). You can further decide to wear it *largo (LAR-go)* (long) or *corto (KOR-toh)* (short).

By combining *largo* and *corto* with the parts of the head, you can describe just about any *corte*. *Largo en los lados (en los LA-dohs)* (on the sides) *y (ee)* (and) *corto en el copete (ko-PAY-tay)* (crown of the head) gives a punk look. *Largo en el copete y atrás (ah-TRAS)* (in back) *y corto en los lados* gives a mowhawk, depending to what extremes your *estilista* takes it.

Ladies may want to go first for a *champú y peinado (chahm-POO ee pay-NAH-doh)* (shampoo and set) to check out a new place at little long-term risk to their image. The *estilista* may ask if you want your *cabello partido (par-TEE-doh)* (parted) *a la izquierda (ah la ees-kee-AIR-dah)* (on the left) or *a la derecha (ah la day-RAY-cha)* (on the right). *El rayo (el RY-oh)* (the part) can be wherever you want it, even *en medio (en MAY-dee-oh)* (in the middle). If you have *un remolino (oon ray-mo-LEE-no)* (a cowlick), you will want to take this into consideration.

Once the ladies have assured themselves of the competence of the employees of a *salón de belleza,* they may want to return for *una base (OO-nah BAH-say)* or *un permanente (oon pair-ma-NEN-tay)* (a permanent). They may even choose to have *un tinte (oon TEEN-tay)* (a tint) put on their *cabello.* If you don't bring along the *tinte* yourself, you can choose the color from a color card. When in doubt, ask if the shade is *rojizo (ro-HEE-so)* (reddish) or *ceniza (say-NEE-sah)* (ash). If the shade you pick is considerably *más claro (mas KLA-ro)* (lighter) than your natural color, they will use *decolorante (day-ko-lo-RAHN-tay)* (bleach) or *peróxido (pay-ROHK-see-doh)* (peroxide). This is not necessary if you want it **más obscuro** *(mas ohb-SKOO-ro)* (darker). No matter what the services you seek at the **salón estética,** with a little looking around and some effort to communicate on your part, you can have terrific looking hair. And even if you make a mistake, it will grow out eventually. In the mean time you can wear a **sombrero** *(sohm-BRAY-ro)* (hat).

Chapter 33

Synonyms:
Sinónimos

In Spanish, as in English, you will find many *sinónimos (see-NO-nee-mos)* (synonyms). These are two (or more) different *palabras (pa-LA-bras)* (words) that mean the same thing. While you may not feel it is necessary to learn all of the ways to say something, it is a good idea to at least recognize the synonyms for common words.

Por ejemplo (por ay-HEM-plo) (for example), there are two common words for "to begin:" *empezar (em-pay-SAR)* and *comenzar (ko-men-SAR)*. The *segunda (say-GOON-dah)* (second) comes from the same root as "to commence" in *inglés*. In addition, there are two more words with the same meaning: *principiar (preen-see-pee-AR)* and *iniciar (ee-nee-see-AR)*. This last looks something like "to initiate" in English, so you might be able to guess its meaning if you saw it written. It is more difficult to detect these similarities when hearing the *idioma (ee-dee-OH-ma)* (language) spoken.

If you are up to it, it is helpful to learn more than one
palabra to say the same thing. This is because most people
who learn a *segundo idioma* speak with an accent.
This can make it *difícil (dee-FEE-seel)* (difficult) for native speakers
to understand you. If you use one *palabra* and get a blank
stare, then you can try *un sinónimo.* It is also important to
try to pronounce *el español* that you know very carefully.
Try to imitate the native speakers that you hear. This will
improve your ear for *el idioma.*

"To finish" is another *palabra* that has several
sinónimos. *Acabar (ah-kah-BAR),* **terminar** *(tair-mee-
NAR)* and *concluir (kohn-kloo-EER)* all mean about the
same thing. You can readily see the similarity between **terminar** and "terminate" in English. But don't pronounce
them the way you would if you were speaking *inglés.* You'll
get that blank expression from the natives, and you'll know
that they *no entienden (no en-tee-EN-den)* (don't understand). Or, *no comprenden (no kohm-PREN-den)* (also
means they don't understand). Here are two more *sinónimos:* **entender** and **comprender.** **Comprender** also has another meaning, which is "to include or contain," as well as
meaning "to understand."

Some words appear to have synonyms, but actually
the *palabras* have different uses. The most obvious *ejemplo*
is **ser** *(sair)* and **estar** *(es-TAR)* which both translate as "to
be." Generally, **ser** is used for characteristics and permanent
conditions—*Emilio es alto (ay-MEE-lee-oh es ALL-toh)*
(Emilio is tall). And **estar** is used to describe location—
estoy en casa (es-TOY en KAH-sah) (I'm at home); tempo-
rary conditions—*estamos bien (es-TAH-mos bee-EN)* (we
are fine); and for the present continuous tense—*usted está
leyendo (oo-STED es-TAH lay-EN-doh)* (you are reading).
In Spanish they are really two entirely different concepts.
Spanish-speakers learning English find it difficult to *comprender* that *inglés* is so imprecise.

Other words that are almost *sinónimos* are **saber**
(sah-BAIR) and *conocer (ko-no-SAIR).* Both translate as "to
know." But *conocer* is used in the sense of knowing a
person or a song—*¿Conoce ese hombre? (ko-NO-say ES-ay*

OHM-bray) (do you know that man?). And **saber** is used to know facts—*¿Sabe cuándo empieza la película? (SAH-bay KWAHN-doh em-pee-AY-sah la pay-LEE-koo-la)* (Do you know when the movie starts?).

Recordar *(ray-kor-DAR)* and **acordar** *(ah-kor-DAR)* are synonyms for "to remember." **Acordar** has the additional meaning of "to reach an agreement or accord"—***Nos acordamos en comenzar el lunes (nos ah-kor-DAH-mos en ko-men-SAR el LOO-nays)* (we agreed to begin on Monday).

Now if you can **recordar** all of these **sinónimos** you will greatly expand your vocabulary. And if you can **acordar** when to use each **palabra** which has an "almost synonym," you will improve your use of **español**.

Understanding more than one word for the same thing will make your comprehension better and using more than one word for the same thing will improve your listeners' comprehension. All this will result in fewer blank looks when you use your **segundo idioma**.

Chapter 34

Humor . . . . .
El Humor

Humor differs from *país (py-EES)* (country) to *país.* And it may be one of the more difficult things to master in *español. Un chiste (oon CHEE-stay)* (a joke) that is funny in *inglés* may not be *gracioso (grah-see-OH-so)* (funny) in Spanish. Sometimes this is because it is a play on words which, when translated, no longer have any relationship. Or sometimes it just falls flat in the other *lengua (LEN-gwah)* (language). Also, *el chiste* is frequently explained in Spanish after it is told. In English, if a joke has to be explained, it usually means that it isn't funny.

Las adivinanzas (las ah-dee-vee-NAHN-sahs) (riddles) are a special kind of *chiste* in the form of *una pregunta (OO-nah pray-GOON-tah)* (a question). Spanish has lots of *adivinanzas,* but even they are different than their English counterparts. Here are a few examples (complete with explanation).

Si el enamorado (see el en-ah-mo-RAH-doh) (If the lover)
es mal correspondido (es mall kor-ray-spohn-DEE-doh) (is spurned, the love not returned)
dígame (DEE-gah-may) (tell me)
el nombre de la novia (el NOHM-bray day la NO-vee-ah) (the name of the girlfriend)
y el color de su vestido (ee el ko-LOR day soo vay-STEE-doh) (and the color of her dress).

This riddle is a little poem. And it is easier to *atinar (ah-tee-NAR)* (to guess) when you see it *escrito (es-KREE-toh)* (written). To decipher it, put together the letters of the second and third words, *el enamorado*, then re-divide after the fifth letter: *Elena / morado*. *El nombre de la novia* is *Elena; el color de su vestido* is *morado (mo-RAH-doh)* (purple). Okay, maybe it's not ready for the Comedy Club. I told you *el humor (el oo-MOR)* (humor) is different in *español*. The next *adivinanza* is similar.

Tengo cinco conejos (TEN-go SEEN-ko ko-NAY-hos) (I have five rabbits)
metidos en un cajón (may-TEE-dohs en oon ka-HOHN) (placed in a box)
¿Cuántos (KWAHN-tohs) (how many)
se quedaron afuera (say kay-DAH-rohn ah-FWAY-rah) (stayed outside)
y cuántos adentro? (ee KWAHN-tohs ah-DEN-tro) (and how many inside?)

Once again, the answer lies in dividing one of the words. Can you guess it? This one is a little more advanced—you have to know the past tense. If the word "placed" (*metidos* from *meter*, to put or fit) is divided, it becomes *metí (meh-TEE)* (I put) and *dos* (two). So, *metí dos en un cajón* (I put two in a box). *¿Cuántos se quedaron afuera?* Three, of course, and two *adentro*. Remember, I started with five rabbits. Beginning to get the hang of it?

This last *adivinanza* is a little different. It is a poem, but it also is a logic problem. It could be translated, but it wouldn't rhyme. That's enough of a hint.

Dos son tres (dos sohn trays) (two equals three)
si puedes ver (see PWAY-days vair) (if you can see)
tres son cuatro (trays sohn KWAH-tro) (three equals four)
si has observado (see ahs ohb-sair-VAH-doh) (if you have observed)
cuatro son seis (KWAH-tro sohn says) (four equals six)
si te fijas bien (see tay FEE-hahs bee-EN) (if you pay close attention)
seis son cuatro (says sohn KWAH-tro) (six equals four)
¡espero (es-PAY-ro) (I hope)
que hayas adivinado! (kay I-ahs ah-dee-vee-NAH-doh) (that you have guessed).

Think about this one for a while. Some people who are strong in logic and math get it, even if they don't speak Spanish. By the way, there is a strong correlation between ability in mathematics and ability to learn a foreign language. Words in a language are symbols which are manipulated by the rules of grammar, in a similar manner to which numbers are symbols manipulated by the rules of algebra and trigonometry.

¿Te das por vencido? (tay dahs por ven-SEE-doh) (do you give up) on the last riddle? Count the letters in each number word. *Dos* has three letters, *tres* has four letters, *cuatro* has six and *seis* has four. *Espero que hayas adivinado.*

Chapter 35

Summer Fun: Diversión De Verano

I n *verano (vair-AH-no)* (summer) when the weather is warm, it is fun to take part in some *actividades (ahk-tee-vee-DAH-days)* (activities). Whether you like to *jugar (hoo-GAR)* (play) at *la playa (la PLY-ah)* (the beach) or in *las montañas (las mohn-TAHN-yahs)* (the mountains), *todos (TOH-dohs)* (all, everyone) will want to get out and *disfrutar (dees-froo-TAR)* (enjoy) *el sol (el sohl)* (the sun).

If your *familia (fah-MEE-lee-ah)* (family) likes *la playa,* don't forget to take along plenty of *bebidas heladas (bay-BEE-dahs ay-LA-dahs)* (iced drinks). *Papá* can *pescar (pays-KAR)* (fish) while *Mamá* and *hermana (air-MA-nah)* (sister) can *bañarse del sol (bahn-YAR-say del sohl)* (sunbathe). But, *¡cuidado! (kwee-DAH-doh)* (careful)! You don't want to *quemarse (kay-MAR-say)* (burn yourself). You want to be *bronceado (brohn-say-AH-doh)* (tanned— end it with an "a" for women).

Los chicos (los CHEE-kos) (the little ones) have *diversión (dee-vair-see-OHN)* (fun) playing in *la arena (la ah-RAY-nah)* (the sand). (Yes, that's the same word we use in English to refer to a ring or stadium. That's because the floor was covered with *arena*—sand. We just pronounce it differently.) Be sure to include *una cubeta (OO-nah koo-BAY-tah)* (a bucket) and *una pala (OO-nah PA-la)* (a shovel) so that they can build *castillos (kah-STEE-yos)* (castles).

En la tarde (en la TAR-day) (in the afternoon), when everyone *tiene calor (tee-EN-ay kah-LOR)* (feels hot), you can *nadar (nah-dar)* (swim) and *jugar en las olas (hoo-GAR en las OH-las)* (play in the waves). *Los chicos* can look for *conchas (KOHN-chas)* (shells) and chase *las gaviotas (las gah-vee-OH-tahs)* (the seagulls).

Tal vez (tall vays) (perhaps) you prefer to take a picnic to *las montañas. Todos* can *montar a caballo (mohn-TAR ah kah-BY-yo)* (ride horseback) and explore the backwoods trails. Wandering down *un sendero (oon sen-DAY-ro)* (a path) in the hills gives you a completely new *vista (VEE-stah)* (view). You'll see *ranchos (RAWN-chos)* (ranches) and *granjas (GRAHN-has)* (farms) and the friendly people who live and work there. You may come across *un manantial (oon mah-nahn-tee-ALL)* (a spring of water) or *un estanque (oon eh-STAHN-kay)* (a pond). Some people like *las montañas* so much that they go there to *acampar (ah-kahm-PAR)* (to camp).

Even if your *horario (oh-RAH-ree-oh)* (schedule) is so full that you can't spare a full day for *la playa* or *las montañas*, you can *disfrutar* a few hours in *el parque (el PAR-kay)* (the park). *Caminar (kah-mee-NAR)* (to walk) in the shade of *los árboles (los AR-bowl-ays)* (the trees) on a warm day in *verano* is *muy relajante (MOO-ee ray-lah-HAHN-tay)* (very relaxing).

There are **columpios** *(ko-LOOM-pee-ohs)* (swings) for *los chicos*. There are **banquetas** *(bahn-KAY-tahs)* (sidewalks) to **andar en bicicleta** *(ahn-DAR en bee-see-CLAY-tah)* (ride a bicycle; the verb means "to walk" also, but when linked with a bike it means to ride) or **patinar** *(pa-tee-NAR)* (to skate). Usually someone nearby is selling **botanas** *(bo-TAH-nahs)* (snacks) or **nieve** *(nee-AY-vay)* (ice cream). You can sit on **una banca** *(OO-nah BAHN-kah)* (a bench) and **platicar** *(plah-tee-KAR)* (chat) or just watch *la gente (la HEN-tay)* (the people).

Remember that to **platicar** is a good way to **practicar** *(prahk-tee-KAR)* (to practice). Wherever you plan your **actividades: en el parque, las montañas**, or *la playa*, take advantage of every opportunity to **practicar** because that is how we learn.

Chapter 36

Place Names: Nombres de Lugares

Many place names in *Alta California (ALL-tah ka-lee-FOR-nee-ah)* (upper California—the state in the U.S.) and throughout the southwestern *EE.UU.* (abbreviation for *Estados Unidos: es-TAH-dohs oo-NEE-dohs)* (United States) are actually Spanish words, reminding us that this area once belonged to Mexico. The many saints honored with cities, *San Francisco* (St. Francis), *San Diego* (St. James), reflect the religious heritage of the early explorers, as do such religious names as *Sacramento (sah-krah-MEN-toh)* (sacrament or Lord's Supper) and *Santa Fe*

(SAHN-tah fay) (holy faith). Other names were politically motivated: **Corona** *(ko-RO-nah)* (crown) and **Reyes** *(RAY-es)* (kings) display adulation for the monarch.

Many names tell us something about the place itself, its geography, its characteristics, or something that happened there. Geographical features noted in their names include **La Ciénaga** *(la see-EH-nah-gah)* (the marsh), **La Sierra** *(la see-AIR-rah)* (the saw or mountain range with peaks like a saw), and **El Cajón** *(el ka-HOHN)* (the box or box canyon). There is also **La Mesa** *(la MAY-sa)* (the table or flat-topped mountain), **La Cresta** *(la KRES-tah)* (the crest of a hill or cock's comb), and **El Prado** *(el PRAH-doh)* (the meadow or lawn).

Some features that relate to bodies of water are **Marina** *(ma-REE-nah)* (seashore), **Laguna** *(la-GOO-nah)* (lake or lagoon) and **Playa** *(PLY-ah)* (beach). In addition, there is **Río Hondo** *(REE-oh OHN-doh)* (deep river) and **Arroyo** *(ar-ROY-oh)* (stream) which may be an **Arroyo Seco** *(SAY-ko)* (dry stream bed) or with water.

Many animals occur in Spanish place names, perhaps because they flourished in the area. There is **El Toro** *(el TOH-ro)* (the bull), **Conejo** *(ko-NAY-ho)* (rabbit), and **Los Gatos** *(los GAH-tos)* (the cats). There is even **Laguna Niguel,** possibly named for the chiggers—**niguas** *(NEE-gwas)*—that bothered the Spanish mapping expedition. If so, the name has been corrupted by the anglo pronunciation of it. **Palomar** *(pa-lo-MAR)* refers to a dove's nest, from **paloma** *(pa-LO-ma)* (dove).

Some names refer to a feature that was man-made. **Ramada** *(rah-MA-dah)* is probably from **enramada** *(en-rah-MA-dah),* a porch or shelter made of **ramas** *(RAH-mas)* (branches). **El Embarcadero** *(el em-bar-kah-DAY-ro)* (the wharf or pier) was a place to embark or get on a ship.

Some names expressed opinions. **La Jolla** or **La Joya** *(la HOY-ah)* (the jewel) and **El Dorado** *(el doh-RAH-doh)* (the golden one) are prime examples. So are **Hermosa** *(air-MO-sah)* (beautiful), **Bonita** *(bo-NEE-tah)* (pretty),

Linda (LEEN-dah) (pretty), and *Chula (CHOO-la)* (cute), all of which have been applied to *playas (PLY-ahs)* and *vistas (VEE-stas)* (views). *Goleta (go-LAY-tah)* (a schooner) falls in the category of something that happened at the place. Doubtless many *goletas* were observed passing this area. *La Crecida (la kray-SEE-dah)* alludes to the swollen state of a river after heavy rains, a condition that does not last in southern California.

Camarillo (kah-ma-REE-yo)(a clique) refers to a close circle of friends. *Bolsa (BOWL-sah)* (a bag or purse) and *Del Amo (del AH-mo)* (the owner's) are pretty clear about what these streets were named for. My personal favorite is *Cucamonga (koo-ka-MO-nah* is the uncorrupted pronunciation—somehow a "g" slipped in over the years). It refers to a hideous mask or to an old hag who is all painted up with too much makeup. I think I've seen one or two of them there.

If you recall how much trouble it was to settle on names for your pets and children, you'll understand how taxing it was on early explorers' creativity to come up with several names for places every day. That's the price you pay when you conquer new worlds. No wonder they resorted to features of the land, occurrences and the religious calendar to help them.

Chapter 37

At the Bank: *En el Banco*

E veryone has occasion to go *al banco* (ahl BAHN-koh) (to the bank) once in a while. Whether you go to *cambiar dinero* (kahm-bee-AHR dee-NAY-roh) (to change money) or to *abrir una cuenta* (ah-BREER OO-nah KWEHN-tah) (to open an account), a little *español* will help you get the service you seek.

If you want to *cambiar dinero*, you will be interested to know *el tipo de cambio* (el TEE-poh day KAHM-bee-oh) (the exchange rate) for the day. The rate can change frequently or remain virtually the same for several weeks. Look for signs with the current exchange rate, or ask the teller, *"¿Qué es el tipo de cambio?"* (kay es el TEE-poh day KAHM-bee-oh?) (What is the rate of exchange?).

There are two prices given: one for buying pesos and one for selling pesos. No matter which you are doing, of the two rates, you will get the one which is less favorable to you and more favorable to the bank. After all, they are in business to make money. *El tipo de cambio* is usually a little better *en el banco* than in *una casa de cambio* (OO-nah KAH-sah day KAHM-bee-oh) (a money exchange house).

If you have some extra *dinero*, you may want to *abrir una cuenta*. You'll have to decide whether you want *una cuenta de ahorros* (OO-nah KWEHN-tah day ah-OHR-rohs) (a savings account) *o una cuenta de cheques* (o OO-nah KWEHN-tah day CHAY-kays) (or a checking account). One consideration is *la tasa de interés* (la TAH-sah day een-tay-RAYS) (the interest rate). Most banks will open either a peso account or a dollar account, but the *tasa de interés* is different for each. You will need to give the teller some basic information: *su nombre completo* (soo NOHM-bray cohm-PLAY-toh) (your full name), *el apellido de su madre* (el ah-pay-YEE-doh day soo MAH-dray) (your mothers surname), *su fecha de nacimiento* (soo FAY-chah day nah-see-mee-EHN-toh) (your birth date), and *su dirección* (soo dee-rayk-see-OHN) (your address) so that *el banco* can send your *estado de cuenta* (es-TAH-doh day KWEHN-tah) (your bank statement). You may have to show some *identificación* (ee-den-tee-fee-kah-see-OHN) (identification) *con su foto* (con soo FOH-toh) (with your photo).

The *empleados* (ehm-play-AH-dohs) (employees) *en el banco* are very helpful and many speak some English. But you will impress them favorably if you attempt to use your *español*. When you come back to *depositar* (day-poh-see-TAR) (to deposit) or to *retirar fondos* (ray-tee-rahr FOHN-dohs) (to take out funds) they will remember you. They might even help you with your *español*!

The Holidays of Mexico

An Abbreviated History

The statues that decorate Mexico's streets and parks often intrigue tourists, as do the patriots on the coin of the realm. Trying to pin-point which historic figure is represented, what he did, and when, can be a real challenge. So here's a thumbnail sketch of some of the high points in Mexican history (and where to find some of the statues).

Cuauhtemoc is fairly easy to spot. He is the only Indian hero who is represented in his native American garb, with feather head-dress and all. A beautiful statue of him is in Tijuana's *Zona Río* at the intersection of *Avenida de los Héroes* and *Bl. Cuauhtemoc*. You pass it if you return from Ensenada on the free road. In 1521 *Cuauhtemoc* succeeded *Moctezuma II*, who had been captured and tortured to death by Cortés. Although he surrendered to the *conquistadores*,

Cuauhtemoc soon suffered the same fate. His short but illustrious career is commemorated on August 13. He also appears on money.

Moving up to 1810, Father Hidalgo initiated the war for Independence on September 16 with the famous *grito* (shout) which is reenacted on this national holiday (see the section on Independence in this appendix). Hidalgo is depicted as a bald man with a fringe of white hair, and wearing a frock coat. He is one of the most popular figures in Mexican history and statuary. He was killed in 1811 and José Maria Morelos continued the fight. Morelos is easy to identify because he is always shown wearing a scarf on his head, a sign among revolutionaries.

In 1857 a constitution was proclaimed which is celebrated each year on February 5. Two years later, Benito Juárez, a Zapotec Indian, became president. His birthday, March 21, is a national holiday. He instituted numerous liberal reforms and his fight against slavery earned him the title of the "Abraham Lincoln of Mexico." His presidency was fraught with unrest.

In 1862 the famous Battle of Puebla took place on May 5. While the French were defeated at Puebla, they still took over the capital and Juárez had to flee for his life. He later returned and the French were finally ousted in 1867.

In 1910 the Revolution began, with Francisco Villa in the north and Emiliano Zapata in the south. Both are portrayed with mustache and bandoleers but Pancho Villa was heavyset and Zapata was slim. November 20 is the national holiday honoring the Revolution (not to be confused with Independence which came one hundred years earlier).

Francisco I. Madero became president but was killed three years later. In 1917 Venustiano Carranza wrote a new constitution and became president. He is the bearded fellow whose likeness appears in Ensenada's *Plaza Civica*.

Skipping ahead to 1938, President Lázaro Cardenas nationalized Mexico's petroleum industry. He thus shocked the world, and didn't win any friends among the foreign businesses that had previously dominated it. But in Mexico he is a hero.

There it is: a brief over view of Mexico's history, correlating holidays, money and statues. Now when you see a statue or the face of a patriot on a coin or bill, you'll know who it is. And when those holidays come around, you'll know what we're celebrating and why the banks and post offices are closed.

La Virgin de Guadalupe

Lady of Miracles

Esteemed throughout Latin America, the Virgin of Guadalupe is known and loved especially in Mexico where she made her first appearance back in 1531. Nowadays her representation appears everywhere: on roadside shrines, on jewelry, even on liquor bottles. And on December 12th she is celebrated in a fiesta, the Day of Our Lady of Guadalupe, *Nuestra Señora de Guadalupe*.

After the Conquest, Fray Juan de Zumárraga, the first Archbishop of Mexico, ordered that all major pagan shrines be destroyed. The deity which had the greatest following near the capital was *Tonantzin*, the goddess of earth and corn, whose shrine was on Tepeyac Hill. The natives were very sad to lose her place of worship.

Early on December 9, 1531, Juan Diego, a poor native, crossed Tepeyac Hill on his way to receive Christian instruction. Suddenly he heard heavenly music and someone calling his name. Then he saw the Virgin, "radiant as the sun." She directed Juan Diego to tell the Bishop that she wanted a church at that spot, exactly where the one for *Tonantzin* had been. She said that she wanted to be near his people to protect and love them, "For I am the Mother of all of you who dwell in this land."

Juan Diego took the Virgin's request for a church to his Bishop, who doubted Juan's story. After the second time Juan went to plea the Virgin's cause, the Bishop demanded a token from the Virgin. But Juan did not see the Virgin the next day; he had to stay home with a sick uncle.

The following day Juan's uncle was so sick that Juan went for a priest to give him the last rites. On his way to *Tlaltelolco* he saw the Virgin again. She spoke to him gently, not angry for his having missed their appointment the previous day. She assured him that his uncle was already well again and instructed him to go to the place where she had first appeared to him and to pick the roses that he would find there. He was to take these to the Bishop. Miraculously, beautiful Castilian roses were growing on the site where only cactus and rocks had been before. Juan Diego obediently picked them and filled his cape with them. Upon seeing the roses, the servants quickly admitted Juan to see the Bishop who immediately believed Juan's entire story.

When the roses were poured from the cape, an image of the Virgin was found on it, another miracle. The Bishop prayed for forgiveness for having doubted, and placed the cape on the altar of the church. Juan Diego pointed out the place where the Virgin wanted the church built and construction was soon underway.

The natives, learning of the miraculous healing of Juan's uncle and the appearance of the Virgin of Guadalupe, became converts in huge numbers. But there was some confusion in their minds between the Christian Virgin of Guadalupe and the Aztec goddess *Tonantzin*, who was also a virgin mother. Their personalities were similar.

Some leading missionaries wanted to abolish the shrine, but the Virgin was so popular and there were so many miracles that she established herself. In 1754 a Papal Bull declared the Virgin of Guadalupe the Patroness and Protectress of New Spain.

During the night of December 11th, people make pilgrimages to the churches of the Virgin. At dawn on the 12th *Las Mañanitas* is sung and dancers in native costume perform for the Virgin. The celebration continues with incense and fireworks. While the largest festival is held at the Basilica of Guadalupe, near Mexico City, there are celebrations all over Mexico, especially in towns with a *Nuestra Señora de Guadalupe* Church.

The 12th of December is a big event in Tecate, where festivities include rodeos and *charreadas* in addition to dancing by people who come from the Las Palmas and La Rumorosa Valleys. Many other towns within easy driving distance of the U.S. also celebrate the day.

Independence

La Independencia

Intense pounding on the door awoke Father Miguel Hidalgo in the wee hours of the morning on September 16. Opening the door, the priest of the village of Dolores was surprised to see Ignacio Allende and a couple of friends from their literary and social club at Queretaro. They pushed their way in so as not to be seen. Father Hidalgo, nearly sixty, was soon informed of the state of affairs that had brought on this late night visit in 1810.

The club at Queretaro, while discussing liberal thought, had formulated the idea that Mexico should no longer be oppressed by Spain nor ruled by Spaniards. They had been approaching key Creole officials and army officers for months, talking to them and winning most of them to their liberal position, aimed at a Declaration of Mexican Independence to be issued in December. But the conspiracy had been betrayed and the Spanish officials had issued orders that its leaders be arrested. The good Father's mind probably flashed back to 1808 when soldiers of the Inquisition had swarmed into Dolores, destroying the trees and vines that Hidalgo had taught his Indian parishioners to plant. He had also taught the Indians simple crafts and to speak Spanish, all in violation of colonial law. Already labeled as defiant, what would the Spanish do to him now?

Known as a humanitarian and a man of great courage, Hidalgo, together with Allende, made an impetuous decision. Rather than flee or wait for arrest, they must rebel immediately. Padre Hidalgo gathered a few followers and arrested the Spaniards in the town.

Then he rang the church bell, summoning the Indians and said to them, "My children, this day comes to us a new dispensation. Are you ready to receive it? Will you be free? Will you make the effort to recover from the hated Spaniards the lands stolen from your forefathers 300 years ago?" And then he gave the *grito* (shout) that inflamed all of northern Mexico and set in motion the War of Independence which raged throughout Mexico for the next eleven years. "Long live independence! Long live Mérida! Down with bad government!" And his parishioners understood and roared back, "Death to the *gachupines* (Spaniards)!"

Armed with knives, slings and clubs, the Indians set off with Hidalgo and Allende to liberate Mexico that very night. In the next village they took an icon of the Virgin of

Guadalupe and this became a banner for what was as much a social revolution as a political rebellion. Upon hearing of the **grito de Dolores**, dozens of towns erupted in rebellion against an oppression which was several times worse than that which had triggered the Revolution in the United States.

After eleven years of bloody fighting filled with courage and heroics, Mexico finally threw off the yoke of Spanish rule. Every year September is the month of *Las Fiestas Patrias* (the Patriotic Festival). Usually in the park or town square people set up booths to sell food and drinks and have games of skill. All month long the tricolor flag is in evidence and patriotism runs high, but most especially on the night of September 15th when there is music, dancing and speeches that build to a climax when the mayor or other honored official gives the **grito**: "*¡Viva México! ¡Viva la independencia! ¡Vivan los héroes! ¡Viva la libertad!*" All of the people crowded into the area, from tiny children on up to adults respond from their hearts, "*¡Viva!*"

This stirring display of patriotism yearly recreates the scene which began the battle for freedom takes place all over Mexico, from small towns to the largest cities. Events begin in the plaza about 8:00 pm, culminating with the **grito** and followed immediately by a huge fireworks display, then dancing and general merriment until the wee hours of the morning.

The actual holiday when no one works and businesses are closed is on the following day, September 16. Nobody would want to work after that kind of celebration! Well worth going to see, it may even move you to shout, "*¡Viva!*"

Cinco de Mayo

The Fifth of May

Cinco de mayo (May 5) is not Independence Day in Mexico, as many mistakenly think. It is the anniversary of the defeat of the French at Puebla, Mexico. Although it is not Independence Day, there are parades and patriotic speeches in many towns.

The invading French army was defeated outside the town of Puebla in 1862 by a valiant band of Mexicans which was far out-numbered and poorly armed. The French still managed to take the capital. President Benito Juárez escaped to the north.

Mexico was not rid of the French until 1867 when Juárez, gradually reclaiming Mexico, regained power and Emperor Maximiliano was executed by a firing squad.

Pancho Villa

Revolutionary Or Bandit?

The anniversary of both the birth and death of one of the most controversial figures of the Mexican Revolution falls in June. Francisco Villa, better known to Americans as "Pancho" Villa, was a brilliant, though unschooled, military strategist. He was a Robin Hood-figure to the common people. He was a volatile and effective, yet barely controllable, ally to key Mexican politicians in an era of upheaval and major reform. Indeed, the Mexican Revolution of 1910 took place during an epoch of romance, when there were causes worth dying for, and you could be whatever you dared to be. Doroteo Arango Quiñonez dared to change his name to Francisco Villa and liberate the state of Chihuahua, where he was governor, albeit briefly. But that's not where his story begins.

On a small ranch named Rancho Río Grande, near the town of San Juan del Río, in the state of Durango, Doroteo Arango was born on June 5, 1878. When his father Agustín Arango died, leaving Micaela Quiñonez Arámburu a widow, the family's economic situation became desperate. Doroteo joined the army. Perhaps memories of his own humble beginnings motivated some of Francisco Villa's later charitable acts. It was as a young soldier that Doroteo met his dear friend Francisco Villa. When his young companion died, Doroteo vowed that his name would not die with him, and so changed his own name to honor his deceased buddy.

Villa's independence and cleverness caused jealousy among some career military men, notably Victoriano Huerta. Huerta, using the pretext of a stolen horse, charged Villa with insubordination and ordered him shot by a firing squad. But Francisco I. Madero commuted the sentence and sent Villa to Santiago Tlatelolco Prison in Mexico City. There in prison Pancho Villa learned how to read. He also learned about the ideals of the agrarian movement, which sought to break up the huge land holdings of the rich and put land into the hands of small farmers. In 1912 Villa escaped prison and fled to El Paso, Texas. The following year, the assassinations of Abraham González and Francisco Madero, the man who had saved Villa's life, impelled him to return to his homeland and fight against the government of Huerta, the man who had sent him to jail.

Villa set up in Chihuahua with a force of only nine men and began to add his actions to the support of the constitutional movement. By May Villa's popularity was evident—he had an army of 600 men. Venustiano Carranza named him Brigadier General as soon as Villa joined the

Guadalupe Plan. Soon the northwest of the state of Chihuahua was under Villa's control. With more victories, the
entire state was his.

In September 1913, Villa was named General in
Command of the Constitutional Army, Northern Division.
He finished the year with a triumphal entry into the city of
Chihuahua. It was at this time that he was named interim
governor of the state. Governor Villa looked out for the
interests of the common people. He seized shops and replaced crooked merchants with honest "administrators."
The markets were filled with the meat of cattle from the
ranches of wealthy land owners and the prices of beans and
meat were lowered. The peasants seldom could afford meat
before this.

Villa expelled from the state any Spaniards accused
of collaborating with Huerta. And he reopened the *Instituto
Científico y Libertario* (Scientific and Libertarian Insti-
tute). He also established the state Bank of Chihuahua and
ordered the printing of currency. The poor people who could
now afford meat and more food were thrilled and delighted
with their Governor's actions. The merchants, Spaniards
and land owners took a different view.

Returning to his role as General Villa, he expanded
his control into the states of Durango and Coahuila. Villa
clearly was in first place among the revolutionary generals.
Then on June 23, 1914, Villa rashly disobeyed Carranza and
marched into Zacatecas. Later, Villa allied himself with his
southern counterpart, Emiliano Zapata, against the constitu-
tionalists.

On March 9, 1916, Pancho Villa and 400 men at-
tacked the U.S. city of Columbus, New Mexico. They re-
treated into Mexico, pursued by General John J. Pershing. It
is said that Villa was a proud man. Some even accuse him of
staging his battles so that hollywood cameramen could film
his troops fighting the revolution, taking advantage of the
best light and the terrain.

When Adolfo de la Huerta assumed the presidency, he insisted upon the surrender of Francisco Villa. On June 26, 1920, Villa signed the Sabinas Pact, swearing to lay down arms and retire to the Canutillo Ranch in Durango which the government had granted to him. Obviously someone did not trust the "Centaur of the North" to stay in retirement. Fearing that he would support the imminent De la Huerta rebellion, Villa was ambushed and killed in Hidalgo del Parral, Chihuahua, on June 20, 1923. In 45 years Francisco Villa, nee Doroteo Arango, had demonstrated himself to be a remarkable military leader, a political force with which to be reckoned, and a hero to the common people from whom he came.

The Day of the Dead

Día de los Muertos

November 2nd, the Day of the Dead, is a national holiday in Mexico. For days before and after, the representation of *La Muerte* (death) can be seen everywhere. Special items are on sale: candies in the form of skulls and skeletons, and macabre toys such as coffins, little funeral processions and dancing skeletons. All this is to help families prepare for the visit of the souls of deceased relatives. The family altar or a special table will be laid out with the favorite foods of the departed.

On November 1st, All Saints' Day, the souls of children who have died are thought to visit the homes. They are expected at night and parents will sometimes set off firecrackers to attract their attention to the right house. Candles and toys are added to the altar for the *angelitos* (little angels). On November 2nd, after the visit of the adult's souls, families visit the grave sites and place flowers on them. Some families have a picnic and make it a social occasion. Vendors are outside the cemeteries to sell flowers, candles and food, and priests are available to bless the graves. After the dead have partaken in spirit of the food set out for them, the living will eat it.

An amusing feature of the Day of the Dead are the verses called *calaveras* (skulls) which appear in newspapers or are sold for a few pesos on loose sheets of paper. They always feature well-known people in public life and give them a satirical eulogy as if they had died. No one is spared, but the humor is all good-natured.

There is so much cultural exchange along the border that many Mexican children dress in costumes on October 31st and go from house to house yelling,"Tricky-tree!" Traditionally the Day of the Dead celebration included an all-night ceremony with candles and fire-works, and food for both the living and the dead. Since elaborate preparations extend the fiesta for several days before the actual event, Halloween incorporates easily into the festivities.

While the sentiments of American Halloween are more similar to *Mardi Gras* or *Carnaval* which Mexicans celebrate before Lent, Halloween does use skulls and skeletons and ghosts for decoration. The Day of the Dead honors the deceased and is an opportunity for Mexican families to decorate graves, remember and console each other. Nevertheless, the two holidays do not contradict each other, and even compliment each other, in much the way that the Mexican and American cultures compliment one another.

Christmas in Mexico

Mexico loves a fiesta, and perhaps the one which is celebrated the longest is Christmas. Throughout December and into January the festive spirit of *Navidad* reigns south of the border. Early in December people begin to decorate their houses with lights and tinsel and the *nacimiento* (manger scene). By December 8th, *Purisima*, or Day of the Immaculate Conception, many tiny lights twinkle in the night and the solemn religious celebration marks the beginning of the Christmas season.

December 16th is the beginning of *Las Posadas*, the traditional pageant re-enacting Joseph and Mary's search for shelter before the birth of Jesus. *Las Posadas* begins nine days before Christmas because it took nine days for Joseph and Mary to travel to Bethlehem, according to tradition.

By December 24th, *La Noche Buena* or Christmas Eve, the festivities are in full swing. A procession to the church for the midnight mass or *Misa de Gallo* will take place all over Latin America. After church there is a huge Christmas feast at each family's home and frequently a *piñata* party for the children who manage to stay awake.

The baby Jesus is added to the *nacimiento* on Christmas eve, and never before. This traditional decoration is treated with great respect and may even be a family heirloom. One patriarch insisted on covering the baby Jesus' face when people celebrating at his house began to dance, "So as not to show disrespect."

Singing is a major part of celebrating Christmas, and in addition to translations of our well-known carols, Mexico has some folk tunes of its very own. One tradition brought over from Spain is the singing of the *coplas*. For this, the whole family begins singing the song, then each member takes turns singing a short, two-line verse as a solo. Everyone joins in the chorus. There are many favorite verses to *coplas*, but people are encouraged to make up verses spontaneously.

December 28th is the Day of the Holy Innocents or *Día de los Inocentes*. It is a festive version of our April Fool's Day. Practical jokes are rampant and anything loaned on this day is considered an outright gift. If someone asks for a closer look at your watch, and you hand it over, they let you know that you have been duped by reciting a short verse.

December 31st there is a party to celebrate New Year's Eve. Americans will feel right at home with the dancing, firecrackers and noisemakers at midnight, and a kiss for your partner. Mexico has some special traditions associated with welcoming the New Year. You may be offered twelve grapes to eat on this night. The grape is a fruit of prosperity, since it never grows alone, but in clusters. Each grape represents a wish for each month of the coming year. Some families remove all suitcases from the house before midnight, representing taking away all the bad luck and misfortunes of the past year. After midnight they bring the suitcases back into the house, filled with good luck and prosperity for the coming year.

Christmas celebrations are not finished yet. In Mexico, gifts are exchanged on January 6th, the Day of the Wise Men or *Día de los Santos Reyes*. Traditionally there have been twelve days of Christmas, beginning with December 25th and ending on January 6th. In Mexico there is almost as much celebrating on *Día de los Santos Reyes*, on the 6th of January as there is on Christmas Day itself. It is believed that on this day the three wise men finally arrived in Bethlehem after their long journey. These kings put gifts for modern children in their shoes, which the kids leave out for this purpose. Much as American children leave a stocking on the chimney for Santa Claus, Mexican boys and girls leave their shoes on the balcony or window sill to be filled with coins, gifts and candy.

Mexican families prepare or have made a special coffee cake to serve on the sixth: the *rosca de reyes*, or wreath of the kings. This circular pastry is served only on this day, and bakeries are flooded with orders for this seasonal treat. Baked inside every *rosca* is a surprise—a tiny figure, representing the baby Jesus. When the cake is served, no one knows who will get the doll. The person who finds the figure in his piece of *rosca* must give a dinner party on February 2nd for all those present on January 6th, usually an extended family and close friends. This is considered an honor.

The second of February is *Día de la Candelaria*, Saint Candelaria Day. In the ecclesiastical calendar, this day was when the baby Jesus was first presented at the temple. The person who got the doll in the *rosca* will buy a larger figure for the party on Candelaria Day. They will dress the doll up like a saint, all in white and with satin if the budget will allow, similar to a child's first communion outfit. This doll will be displayed on the family altar for the day, reminding those at the dinner of the significance of the event. The dinner usually consists of *tamales* and *atole*, a thick hot drink that may be flavored with chocolate or fruit.

So, if you are invited to eat *rosca de reyes* on January 6th, watch out for the doll. There is always lots of joking about anyone who might be too stingy to give the dinner in February—they might even be accused of swallowing the doll to get out of the responsibility! And if you get the little doll, don't be surprised on February 2nd when everyone shows up at your house for dinner!

Surviving South of the Border

The U. S. Consulate

We're all familiar with the old movie scene where an American abroad gets into some kind of trouble and demands to see the U.S. consul. It always seems to end with profuse apologies from important foreign politicians and the American traveler is sped on his way. But how realistic is this? What can a consulate do for you? It's important for you to know beforehand exactly what a consulate can and cannot do to help a U.S. citizen when he is in another country.

Every year Americans make about 30 million trips outside the United States. Moreover, about 1.9 million Americans, excluding military personnel, have chosen to live abroad. The Consulate is the link between these strangers in strange lands and their leaders and representatives back in the U.S. who can mediate on their behalf.

With the exception of a dozen countries with which the U.S. does not have diplomatic relations, there is a consulate in every embassy, in the capital of every country in the world. In addition, many countries, like Mexico, have U.S. consulates located in major cities—Tijuana, for example. More than 250 consulates operate throughout the world just to help us foot-loose and adventuresome types. It's comforting to know that 24 hours a day, 365 days a year you can phone a U.S. Consulate and a duty officer is always available to help a U.S. citizen.

Just what exactly can you expect of them? The consulate will provide the following services:

» They will keep an official record of your presence
   and address in a foreign country.
» They will issue you a new passport if yours is stolen,
   lost, or if it expires.
» They will register the birth of a child and give advice
   concerning dual citizenship.
» They will witness and notarize legal documents.
» They will process veterans' and Social Security
   benefits. (Because these are funds into which the
   worker paid before retirement or discharge, they can
   be paid anywhere. This is not to be confused with
   SSI or welfare which can be paid only in the U.S.).
» They can process income tax forms.
» They will handle registration of absentee voters.
» They will provide information about selective service
   registration.

» They will inform your family at home if you are in financial trouble, have gotten sick, had an accident, or been arrested.

» They will help with legal and practical necessities when a citizen dies abroad.

As you can see, the consulate really can and will do a lot to help when you are in another country. Even as near as Mexico is, it can seem very far away under certain circumstances. The consulate is a communications link between you and your relatives back home. While they can do a lot, there are many frequent requests that a consulate must refuse. Here's what a consulate cannot do:

» The consulate can't provide medical or legal services. However they provide a list of local English-speaking doctors and lawyers.

» The consulate cannot act as an interpreter.

» They will not give out money.

» They will not search for missing luggage.

» They will not settle disputes with hotel managers.

» They will not go after a thief who stole your purse. But if your passport was in it they will issue a replacement.

» They cannot get you out of jail if you are arrested in a foreign country. Everyone is subject to the laws of the country in which they happen to be. A U.S. consular officer can visit an American prisoner to make sure that he isn't being treated worse than other prisoners. That does not mean that he will be treated as if he were in jail in the States.

» The consular officer will also transmit messages to the prisoner's family.

So, the 24-hour emergency number for the U.S. Consulate in Tijuana is not a "Get Out of Jail Free" card. The Consulate in Tijuana is located at 96 Tapachula St. This is the same turn you make off of Agua Caliente Bl. to go to the racetrack. Continue straight ahead three blocks until just before the street ends. The Consulate is the big white building on the right. Their business hours are 9:00 am to 5:00

pm, Monday through Friday. Their regular phone number is (66) 81-7265. Many of the personnel who work there are bilingual. If you are a resident of Mexico, or even a long-term or frequent visitor, it is worthwhile dropping in to let them know where you can be reached. If your family tries to get hold of you and cannot, the consulate will relay a message. Your rich Uncle Alfred's attorney will also be able to find you to give you the inheritance when Uncle Alfred passes on.

To register with the consulate you will need to take your passport or certified birth certificate as proof of citizenship and two photos to the consulate. There you will fill out a form giving your local address and whom to notify in case of emergency. This is a free service and the information is not passed on to any other government office (i.e. the IRS). If you have registered with the consulate and lose your passport for any reason, you will be issued a replacement much more quickly. If you have not registered, it takes about three weeks to get your passport replaced. (Then it is faster to go to the States to apply if you are in a hurry.) The information is shared with other government agencies when you apply for a passport through the Consulate, unlike just registering.

According to Kathy Peterson, director of services at the Tijuana consulate, there are approximately 45,000 Americans living in the area between Ensenada and Tijuana. Of these, only 7000 are actually registered with the consulate. Since the consulate is frequently called upon to identify Americans in case of injury or death, the simple process of registration with them makes their job much easier. Also it can streamline otherwise difficult situations for your family.

Now for that all-important 24-hour emergency phone number: The duty officer for the consulate can be reached at any hour of the night or on weekends and holidays at (619) 585-2000. He will do everything possible to help you, but he is not a magician. There is no substitute for caution and courtesy when you are in a foreign country.

Bargaining Game

Mexico is known as a bargain hunter's paradise, from its economical hotels to its inexpensive gourmet dinners. But many visitors miss out on the greatest international sport since soccer—haggling! By paying the first price that is quoted when inquiring cost, you can miss out on an age-old battle of wits and bluffing: that's the bargaining game.

While not all stores in Latin America allow bargaining, many do. It is fairly easy to tell which stores will not take kindly to your offer of half the amount on the price tag. Some stores display signs that say "Fixed Prices." Others simply look so much like state-side boutiques or department stores, that you feel uncomfortable bargaining. Where price tags are clearly attached to all merchandise you generally do not bargain. International bar code prices on items are a dead giveaway that haggling is not the order of the day. When in doubt, you can always ask if prices are fixed or flexible.

Once you get the hang of haggling, you will grow to appreciate it as the honored pastime that it is. And you will carry home souvenirs that have special memories for you. You'll boast to friends how you paid only half-price for this embroidered shirt and what a steal that intricate wood carving was. And you can save significant money on your gift shopping. No one need know that their present was purchased at a fraction of the cost in a dusty curio shop, and not bought from the gift shop of the New York Museum.

One major drawback to successful bargaining is excessive courtesy. The salesman is not going to try to spare your feelings, so why should you worry about his? This is not to encourage you to be crass and vulgar, but a certain amount of rudeness can work to your advantage. You need not praise the quality of the merchandise—the salesman will do that. In fact, one really gutsy shopper that I know gets great results by stating that it is the ugliest thing of its kind that she has ever seen, but as a favor to the store, and out of her weakness for abandoned mutts and waifs, she will take it (but only at a greatly reduced price!).

The first weapon in the bargaining arsenal is to look poor. Salesmen frequently besiege the obviously well-to-do buyers, leaving the less prosperous-appearing to browse at their leisure. If you are a serious bargain hunter, pack a "shopping outfit:" worn levi's and a tattered backpack are sure signs of a low budget. Leave the designer running shoes and watches at home. That way the clerk is more likely to believe your claim that a given price is beyond your means.

It's a good idea to carry an assortment of bills, especially small ones. Keep your money in different pockets of your clothing, or two or three coin purses and wallets. This way you can pull out a quantity less than the asking price and say, "This is all I have." It can cut down on time spent striking the bargain, and hopefully cut down the price, too.

Where should you start the bidding? Your first offer should be about a third of the stated price, and certainly no more than half. The salesperson may look shocked or offended. That's part of the game. But remember, the two of you are going to gradually work out a compromise, and the higher you start, the higher your final (paying) price will be. Don't get emotionally involved. If you really like something act blasé. You can divert attention from your real interest by idly asking prices for other items during the haggling.

Be prepared to walk away. If the price is not making adequate progress in your favor, make as if to leave. This is a good test of how much the vendor wants the sale, and how close to acceptable your offer is. You may actually have to leave. You can always try again in another store, or go back later. But if the seller lets you leave, your offer was probably way off base. A fresh start later may work out better.

Above all, don't let yourself be manipulated by guilt. Tales of how much raw materials cost, how many children and sick mothers the salesperson supports, etc., are calculated to play on your sympathies. Most of all don't be bullied by the line, "I showed you all this merchandise in different colors and styles, and now you won't buy." Showing merchandise is the salesman's job. If someone else had wanted to buy while he was with you, they would have waited or interrupted.

If you really don't want something, just say, "No." Don't say that it is the wrong color or too expensive. In the intricate language of bargaining that really means yes, you want it. So, if you firmly decide against buying, say "no" and walk away.

By the way, those stores with fixed prices that were mentioned earlier do serve a purpose, even to a dyed-in-the-wool haggler. They will give you an idea of the cost of things before you venture out to make bargains. If a product is not available in the U.S. and you really have no idea of its worth, look for it in a big city department store. This will let you know its value. This is also a good idea, even if you know your U.S. prices—the cost may be significantly different here. The item may be more expensive and not worth the effort to haggle over. Also, these stores frequently will give you a discount for paying with cash instead of credit cards or checks. But you will probably have to ask for the cash discount—it can be as much as ten percent.

One phrase that is particularly useful, whether in a fixed-price store or an open market place: "Is that your lowest price?" You will not offend anyone by asking, and you won't be embarrassed if the answer is "yes." Furthermore, you will often be pleased by a reduced price. Another good ploy is to shop with friends. Many times there is a discount for buying quantities. While you may need only one genuine, life-size replica of the Aztec god of war, your friend might also like to have one, bringing down the prices for both of you.

Remember that bargaining will take time. It is much faster to rush in and pay the first price asked. But you will have a real sense of accomplishment if you take the time to hone your bargaining skills. Also, you will appreciate the skills of the vendors whose profit margin is based largely on their resourcefulness in haggling. Not to mention your pride in the money that you will save! Happy shopping!

Mexico's Own Sport

In spring flowers bloom, gardens are planted, love is declared, and the *charreada* season opens. More Mexican than a bull fight, the *charreada* preserves the tradition of horsemanship, honor, sportsmanship and patriotism that date back to the settling of the land.

The *charro* is one of the most charming and romantic figures in Mexican tradition. He sits high on his horse, wearing his wide-brimmed hat, short jacket and flared pants, all trimmed with silver and braid. His suit is like that worn by the *mariachis,* but this is not a musician. The *charro* maintains Mexico's heritage of fine horsemanship. In fact, the national sport, *Charrería,* was originated at the beginning of this century in an effort to preserve "honor and sportsmanship, fatherland and tradition."

In the coastal zone of Baja California alone, there are thirteen registered *charro* Associations (two of which are located in Rosarito) and seven *Charras Escaramuzas*, made up of young women who excel in horsemanship. This is a very popular and thoroughly Mexican sport. In the area of Tijuana, Rosarito and Ensenada alone, there are 350 *charros* and 70 *Damas Escaramuzas* registered with the *Federación de Charros.*

The legacy of the *charrería* comes from Salamanca, Spain, where the residents of that region are known as *"charros."* The saddle they use is descended from the Spanish saddle which in turn was derived from the Arabic saddle. It was the *Conquistadores* who first brought Arabian horses to North America, where the animals multiplied and thrived. The first *charros* were the land owners and their servants who, on horseback, dealt with untamed cattle. Their activities in cutting, branding and taking cattle to market gave rise to the present-day events, or *"suertes,"* (literally, luck) in a *charreada.*

The *charreada* is similar to a rodeo, but more formal and traditional than its U.S. counterpart. Strict rules govern the way participants dress, even down to the color of the tie the men wear: "The tie shall be in the form of a butterfly (a dangling bow) and in colors of red, brown, gray, or serious color combinations, it being forbidden [to wear] sky blue, lavender, pink, yellow, and other shades improper to the masculine quality of the *charro,"* states the official rule book.

No one may enter the ring without a hat, even the ladies of the *escaramuza* who ride side-saddle. The *charreada* takes place in a *"lienzo charro"* (rodeo ring) which consists of a ring 40 meters in diameter, backed by an expanse of ground 60 meters long by 12 meters wide; seen from above it looks somewhat like a keyhole. There are nine events, or *"suertes,"* each valued with a certain number of points. The *"cala,"* worth 20 points or more, demonstrates elegance, control, posture and strength. The *charro* rides at full speed the 60 meter length of the *lienzo,* reigning in his horse to stop in the exact center of the ring. He then makes the horse do a full turn, half turn, and quarter turn, both to the right and the left. He completes the *cala* by backing his horse to the place in the ring indicated by the judges. You can imagine the long hours of practice that go in to making the *charro* and his horse appear to effortlessly coordinate their movements.

The *"coleadero,"* worth 6 to 12 points or more, demonstrates how a wrangler might bring down a steer if he had no rope—he grabs it by the tail and using his foot, pushes it down. In the *charreada,* this is complicated by first saluting the judges, and having to bring down the beast within a short distance. Points are also awarded according to how the animal falls. Some events are similar to a U.S. rodeo—roping and riding of steers and broncos, for example. But the roping competitions are embellished with fancy rope tricks, such as most Americans haven't seen since Roy Rogers and Gene Autry.

The final *"suerte"* is the "step of death," in which a rider switches from his bareback horse to an unbroken mare while both are moving at top speed. He earns more points (20 or more) if the mare bucks when he mounts her, and if he manages the change of horses at full gallop. (Do not attempt to do this at home; this is done by experts!)

With so many different events, a *charreada* can take several hours. It is a pleasant way to spend a sunny afternoon. There is always traditional music to fill up time between *"suertes,"* and it's not hard to find a vendor with cold drinks and snacks. Like baseball, it is a sport born of a more relaxed era.

Sometimes a team of *escaramuza* will perform. These valiant ladies wear lacy, long, turn-of-the-century style dresses and ride side-saddle. In time to a typical Mexican tune, they put their horses through their paces, riding intricate figures in close formation. Each configuration has a name suggested by the pattern: the wedding ring, the fan, the braid, the stairway. These feminine riders also perform the *"calas!"* Now that's horsemanship! The dainty ladies of the *escaramuza* prove that they can handle their steeds, even in frilly dresses and mounted side-saddle.

If you would like to witness this most Mexican of all sports, ask around in any town in northwestern Mexico. The season runs from April through November at local *lienzos*. Worth seeking out, you will be rewarded with pageantry, tradition, music, skill and horsemanship. It's a fine day's entertainment!

The Music of Mexico

Mexico has one of the largest and most varied musical repertoires of any country in the world. Her national styles of music differ widely, from the strident strains of the *mariachis,* to the strangely limping rhythm of the *cumbia,* to the sweet serenade of the romantic trios, not to mention the lively *ranchera* music of the Mexican cowboy that seems to grate on gringo ears. For Anglo listeners, the type of Mexican music which appears easiest to appreciate is that of the romantic trios. It has some characteristics which have been popular in U.S. music, yet combines them with distinct foreign elements in a pleasing way.

Many Americans tend to call any strolling musicians in Mexico *"mariachis,"* but this is not correct. The *mariachis* are the guys in the *charro* suits—wide-brimmed *sombreros,* short jackets and tight pants, all trimmed with silver and braid. There are usually at least five of them, but may be as many as fifteen or more. Their instruments include guitars, **guitarrón** (a big, bass guitar), violins and trumpets.

The **conjunto norteño** is usually three or more musicians whose costumes are levis, western-style shirts, and cowboy hats and boots. They are the only strolling musicians who include an accordion and snare drum, along with the ever-present guitar and possibly a **guitarrón**. Unless you are a truly seasoned "Mexiphile" or a real lover of **ranchera** music, I advise most visitors to pass on this **conjunto**. Their music is an acquired taste, even for fans of American cowboy music.

The third kind of strolling musicians seen in Mexico are the romantic trios. This is, of course, three men, usually dressed in business suits. But their unremarkable style of clothing belies the beautiful music which they produce. Their instruments include a **requinto** (a small guitar strummed sort of like a mandolin), one or two guitars, and/or some kind of hand-held rhythm instrument, like **maracas** or **claves**. The **tríos románticos** are the musicians who produced what has come to be known as Mexico's golden age of music in the '30s and '40s. But this style of music is never out of fashion, even today. They sing in close harmony, like barber shop quartets, but their music is set to exotic beats like the **bolero** the **son** and the **bossa nova**. They also sing to such familiar rhythms as the foxtrot, ballad and waltz, and even a sweetly-intoned, tamed down **ranchera** now and then. The style is largely a method of interpretation lending itself to many songs. You may even recognize American favorites like "The Way We Were," translated and sung in three part harmony.

The highest voice is frequently a contra-tenor, and may be mistaken for a woman's. But traditionally all of the strolling musicians are men. Nevertheless, Edie Gorme had great success recording several of the songs of romantic trios. The music of the trios is especially good to accompany dinner or an evening of conversation. Most of the music of the **mariachis** and **conjuntos norteños** is too strident for this. It lends itself more to drinking, partying and sometimes dancing. A happy patron occasionally staggers to his feet to sing along, with feeling. But not with romantic trios; theirs is easy-listening *a la mexicana.*

So, when you come upon a romantic trio, what songs can you request? Literally, there are thousands. If you can't remember specific titles, you can ask for songs by famous groups: *Los Tres Ases, Los Panchos, Los Tres Caballeros,* or *Los Dandys.* Or, you can choose songs from the following list. Some will be familiar, others may be new to you. But all will give relaxed listening pleasure to visitors' ears. The list is by no means exhaustive, but it gives you a place to start to enjoy this beautiful style of Mexican music.

Nuestro Amor
No Me Quieres Tanto
No Trates De Mentir
Amorcito Corazón
Un Siglo de Ausencia
Una Copa Más
Solamente Una Vez
La Gloria Eres Tu
Noche No Te Vayas
Quizás, Quizás, Quizás
Ya No Quiero Verte
Tu, Ni Te Lo Imaginas
Como Un Madrigal
Vereda Tropical
Ojos Verdes
Parece Que Fue Ayer
Contigo Aprendi
Noche De Ronda
Presentimiento
Mil Violines
Sin Ti
Ella
Sin Un Amor
Júrame

Cuarto Vidas
Amor Indio
Somos Novios
Amapola
Preciosa
Alma Mía
Luciérnaga
Silencio
Peregrina
Caminemos
Odiame
Luz De Luna
Novia Mía
Perfidia
Mona Lisa
Tres Regalos
Caminante
Candilejas
Negrura
Bésame Mucho
Cerca Del Mar
Abrázame
Rayito De Luna

"Peregrina," The Romantic Pilgrim

Mexicans have a flare for romance, and nowhere is it more clearly evident than in their music. The ballad *"Peregrina"* is a classic example. It is not only romantic in its lyrics, but also in the story of how it came to be written. The first stanza praises the beauty of the lady to whom it is sung: "Pilgrim with pale, divine eyes and cheeks lit up with blush ... Your hair is as radiant as the sun." That's guaranteed to get her attention!

The next stanza comments how she has left her home in a cold climate to come to this tropical land. The words go on to say that the songbirds of the meadows sing their tunes for her and the perfumed flowers caress her lips and forehead. In the final stanza the singer begs the "pilgrim with the enchanting face" when she leaves his land, "Do not forget my land, do not forget my love." Certainly the words are enough to sweep even "Hard-hearted Hannah" off her feet!

The music is slow and haunting. And it is one of the few Latin songs written especially for a blonde or fair-skinned lady. The words for *"Peregrina"* were written by Luis Rosado Vega and the music by Ricardo Palmerín, who were commissioned to write the song in 1918 in the midst of a socialist rebellion in Yucatán. Felipe Carrillo Puerto, governor of the state, had fallen in love with Alma Reed, an

American reporter who had been sent to cover the political situation. She was young and beautiful and although she spoke no Spanish, she quickly captured the heart of the man who had recently lead his party to take over the peninsula.

Some of Palmerín's best songs came out of this era. He and Rosado Vega had previously collaborated on tunes. Yet, even though Palmerín completed more than three hundred songs in his lifetime, *"Peregrina"* was his most successful, attaining international acclaim. Carrillo Puerto went to Palmerín and asked that he compose a song that would tell Alma of his love for her and ask her to stay in Yucatán or, if she must leave, to return and stay forever.

For the premier performance of this work, Carrillo Puerto held a party for close friends, including Alma Reed, at the Mayan ruins at Chichen-Itza. There, in front of the Temple of the Soothsayer and under the light of the tropical moon, Palmerín and Galay, a tenor, sang *"Peregrina"* for the first time in public. Those present were electrified by the beauty and sentiment of the song rendered in such a magical setting.

History does not record whether Alma returned to Yucatán and to Felipe Carrillo Puerto. Perhaps this is due to a gentleman's discretion. The song has been sung to "pale eyed beauties" thousands of times since that first moonlit night, here again with unknown results. Lots of musicians specialize in romantic music, both dance bands and strolling trios. If you want to know the effect of the song, some night request *"Peregrina."* And if the moon is shining just right... who knows what might happen.

Mariachis

The dashing *mariachi* bands that play the beautiful traditional songs of Mexico are an integral part of any celebration. Decked out in their *charro* outfits, these handsome musicians in their wide-brimmed hats can be seen in some restaurants as well as at private fiestas. And what girl can resist a romantic serenata when her boyfriend brings a *mariachi* band to her house at midnight? That will make any *señorita* smile and throw a rose from her balcony.

At parties the music may be provided by the host, but in public settings the *mariachis* are "free lancing." That is, they expect the person requesting a song to pay for it. Live music does not come cheap. They average between fifty cents to a dollar (U.S.) per musician per song, the price depending on the experience and size of the band. So if you are confronted by a group of eight mariachis, the price will be between $4.00 to $8.00 per song. They can be hired by the hour for prices ranging from $100.00 to $150.00 (U.S.). As you can see, this is not like putting quarters in the jukebox, but you get quality music, interaction with the performing artists, and they play requests. However, ask the price before getting yourself into an embarrassing situation.

Did you ever wonder what the guy at the next table said to the *mariachis* to get them to play such a beautiful tune? There are thousands of melodies in the repertoire of Mexico's traditional music! Unfortunately, most non-Mexicans know only a few titles to request, resulting in a boring evening for both musicians and patrons. Beyond *"Guadalajara"* and *"El Rancho Grande"* is a whole wonderland of songs. And if *"La Cucaracha"* is the only song you can think of, perhaps you had better let someone else make a request.

Songs played by mariachis can be divided into four basic categories: 1) courting songs, 2) sad love songs, 3) hometown, the Revolution and horses, and 4) instrumental. Try listening to the songs, really paying attention, and you may soon develop a taste for this kind of music. The harmonies and rhythms are sometimes different from American music, but fascinating.

If you speak Spanish you will be enchanted by the message of each song. They seem to have a wider range of musical subject matter than American music. Even if you don't understand all the words, you can certainly tap your feet and applaud. Herewith is a list of songs familiar to most *mariachi* groups. Each band has its own repertoire and may not know every song, but there are enough to keep any group busy for quite a while. Memorize the names of one or two and impress your friends next time you are out. Or, take this book along. This is not a complete list—there would not be room here. It is only a beginning to introduce you to a wider range of songs. From here the possibilities are almost limitless.

» Courting songs:
Golondrina Consentida (The Swallow)
Féria de Las Flores (Fair of the Flowers)
Cuatro Caminos (Four Roads)
Vámonos (Let's Go)
Solamente Una Vez (Only Once)
Gina (Gina)
Buenas Noches Mi Amor (Good Night, My Love)
Los Laureles (The Laurel Trees)
Son De La Negra (The Brunette's Dance)
» Sad love songs:
Albur De Amor (Dawn of Love)
No Volveré (I'll Not Return)
Tres Días (Three Days)
Paloma Negra (Black Dove)
Déjeme Llorar (Let Me Cry)
Cenizas (Ashes)
Ella (Her)
Por Un Amor (For Love)

Que Les Vaya Bonito (May Things Go Well)
Le Solté La Rienda (I Gave You Free Rein)
Cruz De Olvido (Cross Of Forgetfulness)
Simón Blanco (Simon Blanco)
Las Rejas No Matan (Iron Bars Don't Kill)
» Hometown, the Revolution and horses:
Canción Mixteca (Mixtec Song)
Caminos De Michoacan (Michoacan Roads)
Caballo Prieto Azabache (Jet Black Horse)
El Caballo Blanco (The White Horse)
Chapala (Chapala)
El Rey (The King)
La Fiesta De Vaquilla (The Branding Party)
Mi Amigo, El Tordillo (The Dapple Gray Horse)
» Instrumental:
El Niño Perdido (The Lost Child)
Coronelas (The Colonel's Wife)
Zacatecas (Zacatecas)
La Culebra (The Snake)
El Zopilote Mojado (The Wet Buzzard)
Los Machetes (The Machetes)
Camino Real de Colima (Colima's Royal Highway)

A Musical Geography Lesson

One of the most popular songs in the north of Mexico is *"El Caballo Blanco"* or "The White Horse." This lively song is a good example of the *corrido,* a folk ballad that tells a story, and at the same time is a sort of musical geography lesson about the northwestern coastal states. Most *mariachi* groups know it and sing it with gusto whenever asked.

There are dozens of *corridos.* The word is sometimes said to derive from the verb *correr,* to run, because this type of song seems to run on and on. The word may also be derived from *ocurrido,* a happening or occurrence, because most *corridos* are a retelling of some important event, or of what happened to a particular person. They are even spontaneously composed for special occasions, including elections and other newsworthy events.

The music consists of a simple melody repeated until the complete story has been told. These songs once served to spread news in remote villages, but because of satellite communication, this function of the song is passing away. Still, the *corridos* commemorate battles, murders and catastrophes.

The *corrido* of the White Horse is less gruesome—it celebrates the rapid journey of a particular horse from Jalisco to Baja California. It is unknown why the horse had to make the trip so fast; there is no mention in the song of a race, or if the rider carried important news or was fleeing. But the lyrics tell how he left Guadalajara one Sunday for the north. Most of the song mentions the names of the towns through which the horse passes, giving us a chance to cheer for our own town when it is named.

In the second verse the rider takes off the reins and saddle and rides bareback "like lightening" through Nayarít. Then the singer has a choice whether the horse passes through Escuinapa or El Rosario, Sinaloa. It can be sung either way, and musicians try to choose the town which will please their audience.

The horse and song continue on through Culiacán, and by the time they reach Los Mochis the horse is nearly falling from exhaustion. The horse recovers some in the Valle del Yaqui located between Ciudad Obregón and Guaymas, and in spite of being lame, he continues the adventure. He goes on through Hermosillo and Caborca, Sonora, and feels like dying by Mexicali. Still he climbs La Rumorosa, arriving in Tijuana by the dawn! This is probably where the song ended before the influx of population to the peninsula. In order to appeal to the residents of Baja, another verse was added. It says that although his task was finished, the horse went on to Rosarito and "Didn't want to stop until he saw Ensenada."

So there you have it: a geography lesson guided by a horse in a folk song, that covers five states and more than 1500 miles. *El Caballo Blanco* is certainly worthy to be celebrated in his own corrido. People throughout the northwest of Mexico love to hear his story sung.

Now to add to the mystery of the lyrics—some people say it wasn't a horse at all. It was a car named for a horse, like a pinto or mustang. It gives you something to think about when you listen to the words. And don't forget to cheer when they mention your town!

Appendix of Slang Terms

Irresponsible Moral Disclaimer

This appendix contains a wide range of slang terms, including what some would consider vulgar; it seemed pointless to omit phrases that are commonly heard. The words contained here have been heavily edited to attempt to offend fewer readers (if you want the real dirt, get Bueno Books' **Mexican Slang**). This is not to advocate that readers run around foreign countries spewing nasty words, (and if you are offended by coarse language, read no further) but it is helpful to know what is meant by words that one hears— and to know what words to avoid repeating. Translators and interpretors find this section especially helpful, since the proper Spanish which they learned in school is not necessarily what the man-on-the-street speaks. To that end, questionable words are categorized by the kind of company in which they are acceptable. "Polite" means acceptable in any company, "acceptable" means in mixed company of sophisticated adults.

Aside from terms that may be crude, there are others which may have street connotations that would sound like "gutter talk" in polite company. Others are youth slang and as such can make your speech sound hip to some or silly and juvenile to others. It is a good idea to ask someone privately when in doubt. If you commit a *faux pas*, simply apologize; you are not a native speaker, after all.

Keep in mind that words change meaning in different countries. To call a man *cabrón*, for instance, is common and relatively tame in Mexico, but in Cuba and some other countries it means that you have cuckolded him, and is a grave insult capable of turning a friend into an enemy instantly. It is best to be careful of insults, even playful ones.

Linguistic Notes

We assume that readers already have a basic command of Spanish. If not, get one before you run around spouting slang. Ordering *dos chelas* instead of *dos cervezas* is no big deal, and can give you panache, but speaking more slang than Spanish will only make you look like an idiot.

Likewise, we assume you are familiar with Spanish pronunciation and are aware of gender endings. (If guys are *chavos*, chicks are *chavas*, if a bald man is *pelón* a bald woman is a *pelona*, old men are *viejitos*, old women *viejitas*, etc.) We also assume you can conjugate Spanish verbs, which are presented here in the infinitive form. (If not, just use the infinitives—you'll sound primitive, but will be understood.)

Hip American Expressions, Translated

COOL

A major expression with many synonyms in both languages.

Padre

Is the most direct equivalent, as in "He's a really cool singer," *Es cantante muy padre*. Can be used impersonally, like "Far out!" *¡Ay, que padre!* Extremely cool would be *padrísimo*.

Curado

Similar to *padre* but hipper. Probably comes from the pun of *padre* meaning *cura* (priest).

Suave

While it means "smooth" or "soft," *suave* also has a definite equivalence to "cool" and *suavecito* is cooler yet. The Camel Filter "cool character" billboards in Mexico say *Un Tipo Suave*.

Chingón

A tougher, more masculine, street connotation, it could describe a car, motorcycle, or person and might be thought of as meaning "stud." Not polite, but highly visible on T-shirts and caps. *Que coche más chingón* is "What a cool car."

Chido

Means "cool" or "bitchin'" in urban gutter talk, but is getting to be a popular term with "yuppies."

Estar de pelos

Hip, youth slang. Something like "rad" or "too much." *La camisa está de pelos* is "The shirt is way cool." A variation is *"pasar de peluche." Peluche* is fleece and *un osito de peluche* is a teddy bear. The very latest "Youthspeak" as we go to press is *de pelos y jícamas.*

Simpático

Means "nice," especially of people. Nice people are also *bonito, lindo, buena onda. Él es gran tipo* means "He's a great guy." You could also say, *¡Que tipazo!*—"What a guy!" In fact, the use of the *-azo* ending, which implies a blow with or explosion of the word modified, is good for homemade slang. We recently heard a woman summon a good looking young waiter by calling, *"Jovenazo."* Impersonally, *bonito* is literally the diminutive of "good," and means "nice." *Que bonito* is "How nice."

Caer Bien

To be *simpático. Él me cae bien* is the way to say such things as, "I like him," "He's all right," "He's cool with me." Better usage than *me gusta* when discussing people—especially people of the same sex.

Prendido

Prender means to turn on a light or light a fire, so something *muy prendido* is a real turn-on. *Me prende* means "it turns me on."

Bárbara

Means "barbaric," but as an exclamation means, "Way cool," "Far Out," etc. But *Que barbaridad* (which comes from the same root) means, "What a bummer" or "Disgraceful." Additionally, *una barbaridad de* means "a lot of," yet *cuesta una barbaridad* means "it costs an arm and a leg." Go figure.

Tranquilo

Means calm or serene, but is also "cool" in the sense of "cool it," "chill out," or calm down. Can be used as a one-word imperative. *Calmada* is similar to *tranquila* and *la cosa es calmada* or *toda calmada* means "everything's cool."

UNCOOL

Feo, Gacho

Feo means ugly, but is used in many deprecative senses, road conditions, weather, behavior, music, can be *feo*, so it could mean, "lousy," "in bad repair," etc. Used impersonally, *feo* has sense of "a drag," "a bummer." Used about a person, it means "ugly," unless applied to certain characteristics: *Tiene carácter feo* means "He's got a rotten character." *Gacho* is street slang and has all the same connotations. Can be used personally or impersonally; *¡Que gacho!* means "Bummer" or "What a drag." *Eres gacho* means "You stink." *No seas gacho* is "Don't be a drag" or "Come off it."

Pesado

Literally means "heavy," but has a negative connotation in slang, very *antipático*. Generally applied to a person. Can mean boring, a drag, a creep. Also *pesadito*. Other terms include, *sangrón*, *peseta*, *caer en los huevos*, *chocante*. One frequently hears *No seas sangrón*, or *No seas pesado* for "Don't be a pain."

Chingado

Screwed up, jerked around, as in the T-Shirts that say *Estoy chingado*.

Caer Gordo

Literally, "to fall fat," this is the opposite of *caer bien*. *Ella me cae gorda* means, "I don't like her," "she's a bummer," "She rubs me the wrong way." If you want to use an expression which is less slangy try *caer mal*.

Fuchi

Stinky, smelly. But by extension, anything corrupt, perverse, kinky, or not to the liking. As an exclamation, means "Phew!" or "Yuck!" Also *fu* or *furris*.

¡Guácala! also means "Ugh!" "Yech!" "Gross!" or "Barf!" but is more about taste than smell. The comment is *de rigueur* when spitting something out on the floor.

Asombroso

Though it actually comes from the root *sombra* and literally signifies "overshadowing," it curiously means what it sounds like—"awesome."

FUNNY

Chistoso

From *chiste*—a joke. Means "funny" in the sense of comical, someone who jokes a lot. Other words for "joke" include *broma* (and the verb *bromear*) and *cotorro*. In Spanish, incidentally, there are no "dirty" jokes, but *chistes colorados* for "blue" material and *chistes verdes*, which are "sick" or off-color jokes. *Raspa* is a bad joke or pun (pun is *albur*, the verb *alburear*).

Gracioso

Also funny, as in "Very funny,"—*muy gracioso* or "What's so funny"—*¿Qué tiene de gracioso?* A noun as in *¿Quién fue el gracioso?* (Who's the wise guy?) A humorous person; indicates natural humor more than formal joking.

Vaciado

Slang term, meaning funny in the sense of "a kick" or something that tickles one. "It's a scream that your mom likes rock music," would be *Que vaciado que le gusta el rock a tu mami*. Not related to *vacilar*, to joke around.

Burlar

To joke or kid around. *Burla* is a joke, prank, or jest. (Differs from *chiste* as telling a joke differs from an April Fool jest). "You're kidding" is *Me burlas*. "Don't put me on" would be *No te burles*. A joker or "card" would be described as *burlesco*.

Picarón

Picar means to sting, pick, or bite, like a mosquito, but the word has wide application. "Hot" food, for example is *picante*. "Is this *salsa* very hot?" would be ¿*Pica mucho?*

Picarón is a joker, a "card," the thing to call someone who's just put one over on you or told a good one. The sense is more towards barbed or racy humor and *picaresco* means exactly that—a song with *letra picaresca* is a racy or sexy one.

Payasear

Fooling around, clowning around, kidding. *Payaso* means "clown." "Just kidding" would be *Nomás estoy payaseando. No seas payaso* would mean "Cut the clowning."

Caer el veinte

To "get" a joke can be expressed as *caer el veinte*, referring to the 20 *centavo* coins used in telephones, and equivalent to our expression, "the coin finally dropped." *Por fin le cayó el veinte* means "He finally got it." *Caer* (to fall) by the way, is the way of expressing "fall for it." *Caíste* means "You fell for it" or "Gotcha!" *No cayó* means "He didn't bite."

Tomar los pelos

Literally (taking the hair), this means "pulling my leg." ¿*Estás en serio o me estás tomando los pelos?* would mean "Are you serious, or are you pulling my leg?"

Raro

The English use of "funny" to mean "odd" or "peculiar" does not follow in Spanish. "That's odd" would be *curiosa* and "weird" is *raro*. "This soup tastes funny" would be *Esta sopa tiene un gusto raro*. *Tipos raros* are strange people or weirdos.

FOXY

(All these can be used with *bien* to mean "pretty cute," "really foxy," etc). *Guapo* is handsome, *guapa* is foxy. Both can be used as an address; (*Hola, Guapo* means "Hello, Handsome"); or as a noun (*Hay muchas guapas* would mean "There are a lot of foxes around.) Other adjectives that can be feminized by changing the final "o" to "a" are *lindo, bonito*, and *buen mozo* (good looking). Only men are referred to as *cuadrado*—"built" or "buff."

Women can be *cuero*—"stacked" or "built." Women can be cute—*preciosa* or *mona*, pretty—*chula*, beautiful—*bella, hermosa*, or gorgeous—*primorosa*. A beauty is *un primor*, or *una belleza*. Good looking women are called, *cuerito* and *cuerazo, buenota, buena curva, guitarra* (from the shape of a guitar), *mango*, and alley terms *forro* and *forrazo*.

Perita en dulce (pear in syrup) can mean a "wannabe," or chick who thinks she's gorgeous. Ugly women are called *garra* (claw), *piedra* (stone) or perhaps *pellejo* (rawhide or an animal skin).

BREAD, DOUGH

Most common slang for money in border areas is *feria*, which can mean "money" or "pocket change," depending. *No traigo feria* would indicate, "I don't have any change." Further south, one hears *lana*, which literally means "wool."

The term *plata* is understood to mean *dinero* throughout Latin America, but in Mexican border areas occasionally means *pesos* as opposed to dollars. One also hears *¿Y cuánto en inglés?* for "How much in dollars?" Other words for money: *pachocha, marmaja, luz.*

De lana means rich, so you hear odd phrases like *torta de lana* which means, not "wool sandwich," but a rich chick.

Mendigo means "beggar," but when accented on the first syllable becomes a deprecative adjective similar to "darned" or "cotton picking," or a noun similar to *cabrón.*

While *barata* is cheap, used as a noun it means a sale or bargain, as does *ganga*. Better yet would be *de balde* or *de oquis*, which mean "for free." *Abono* might be fertilizer but *en abonos* is installments or time payments (differing from *sistema de apartados*, which is "lay away") and would require an *enganche* (hook), or "down payment." A common Mexican phenomenon is *pilón*, a bonus or extra value offered in business, like an extra donut in the dozen or a free month's rent.

Caifás is street slang for "pay up" and *caifás con mi lana* is "cough up now." A similar phrase is *azota mi lana* (literally, "whip me my dough"). *Chambear* means "to work," *chamba* or *jale* mean job, or gig. A salary can be called *chivo* (he-goat) or *raya* (line or scratch), while a child's weekly allowance is his *domingo.*

Droga means "debt" as well as "drug," so terms like *droguero* and *endrogado* have secondary meanings of "heavy borrower" and "debt-ridden." *Apuro* is a financial bind and "broke" can be *pelado* (peeled), *jorobado* (hunchbacked), or *brujo* (witch or sorcerer). *En la quinta* is to be in total poverty or misery, like "in the poorhouse."

GIMME A BREAK

An almost literal translation would be the expression, *Dame chanza*. Street slang uses *Alviáname* to bum anything from cigarettes to favors. A similar usage is *mochate*, for mooching. *No seas gacho, carnal. Alviáname. Mochate un frajo*, would be, "Be a sport, brother. Gimme a break. Spare me a cigarette."

SHIT

Mierda is the common term and not used vulgarly as in English (where some use it for everything). *Caca* is the same in Spanish as in English, again without any other meanings. Also heard is *popó*. *Cagar* is the crude verb for defecating, *zurrar* even cruder; so *cagón* and *zurrón* both mean a shitty person. *Cagadero* means "crapper."

Miar is a cruder term for peeing than *orinar* and *mingitorio* is a pisser. Piss is also *chis* or *pipí* and saying something like *Tengo que hacer pipí* is an inoffensive way of saying you want to pee. *Chorro* is crude for diarrhea and *grifo* (faucet) cruder yet.

"Bullshit" would be most politely translated as *mentiras* (lies), or perhaps the slangier *macanas* or *chucherías*. *Déjate las macanas* means, "Cut the B.S." *Carambas* is used as a synonym in the since of "giving someone a hard time."

The term *basura* (garbage) is used more widely in Spanish and a mess, disaster or bad meal would be a *porquería*, as would a messy house or room. One would say, *¡Ay, qué cochina!*

HIP, WITH IT

C *ojonudo* means "ballsy," but also means, "with it," as does the old expression *muy reata* (very lariat).

Oddly, while *muy acá* (real "here") means "hip" in most of Mexico, at the border and in the U.S. one hears *muy de aquellas* (real "there") to mean "way out" or "out of this world." Any of these expressions can be inflected to mean *creido* (believer), which is the Spanish way to say somebody thinks themself to be a big deal.

TOTALLY, TO THE MAX

R *emate* is an auction, but has a slang sense of "all the way," so *un loco de remate*, for instance is a total nut. Another expression, *de hueso colorado* (red-boned) means dyed-in-the-wool, totally, last ditch, a diehard. It's often used to describe team fans or political partisans and a phrase like *Soy Mexicano de hueso colorado* is not too different from "red blooded American." Doing something "all the way out" or "full bore" is *a todo dar*, the slang version being *a todo madre.*

Hip Mexican Expressions

T*engo madre muy padre, y padre de poca madre.*

Madre

This is a complex word in Mexico and produces a major amount of rich slang. Without getting into the sociology of it, although the concept of Motherhood is held sacred in Mexico, *madre* means worthless, failed, a mess. *Una madre* is something unimportant, a put-down; *un desmadre*, is a total snafu. A *madrazo* is a heavy blow or jolt, a *madreador* or *madrino* is a bar bouncer, hit man, or goon. *Partir la madre* is to smash, destroy, or bust something. The classic Mexican insult (the equivalent of "Screw you") is the famous *Chinga tu madre* or merely *Tu madre*.

Exceptions to all this maternal negativity are *a todo madre*, which means done right, superlative, done up brown, the whole nine yards; and *No tiene madre*—if something "has no mother" it is absolutely the coolest. However, and to illustrate the importance of context in such elemental slang, *Él no tiene madre* can also mean having no shame, so that *poca madre* is also a synonym for "jerk" (*poca abuela* avoids the crude use of the word *madre*).

Me vale madre, frequently seen on caps, shirts, and biker jackets, literally means "It makes mother to me," but is a direct equivalent to English expressions such as "I don't give a damn," or "Who gives a shit?" *Madre* used like this is considered crude speech and not acceptable in polite or mixed company, so there are euphemisms. People will say things like "*a todo M*" (like we would say, "the M word"). More transparent are such as *drema*, and the similarly scrambled *la ingada chadre*.

Chingar

This is another major plexus of Mexicanisms, and more complex than most non-Mexicans think. *Chingar* does not mean precisely "screw," but comes from an older meaning of "rape" or "molest." While *No chingues con nosotros* is equivalent to "Don't mess with us," the famous *Chinga tu madre* is not sexual at all (worse, to a Mexican). *Hijo de la chingada* is "son of a bitch," but in spades. *Vete a la chingada* is rougher than "go to hell," more like "get screwed" in its stronger phraseology.

Hasta la quinta chingada means a long distance, "way the hell out," and can be shortened to *hasta la quinta*. A *chingazo* or *chingadazo* is a major blow or coup. *Chingadera* is a dirty trick. *Me chingaron* means "I got screwed" or "jerked around" —"they did me." *No chingues* is "lay off" or "don't fuck around."

Chingón is a compliment—a stud, the guy who can *chinga* everybody else. *Un chingo de* means a whole lot of, as in *Hace un chingo de años, Colón descubrió las Américas* (A whole heap of years ago, Columbus discovered America). The primacy of these *chinga* terms has led to a lot of expressions and ejaculations like *¡Chin!*, *¡Ay, Chihuahua!*, *¡Chispas!*, *¡Chicle!*, which are acceptable bailouts, just as we have all the "Gosh" and "Golly" words to prevent blasphemous use of "God."

Although *fregar* means cleaning or scrubbing in most Spanish countries, in Mexico it is a synonym for *chingar* in the sense of "messing with" or "bugging." *Fregado* means "snafued" or "screwed up" and *No me friegues* is "Don't bug me." A euphemism used in place of the various forms of *chingar* is *tiznar*.

La Onda

A constellation of sixties hippy expressions which are still quite current. *Onda* means vibrations, so *¿Que onda?* is something like, "What's the vibes?" and is the standard young, hip greeting, as ubiquitous as "What's happening?"

Buena onda, whether referring to a person or impersonal thing or event means "Good vibes." *Ella es muy buena onda* means "She's great people." Conversely, *¡Que mala onda!* means "What a bummer!" Though not as often heard, *otra onda* can mean "something else" as in "Man, that band was something else."

Huevos

This is another complex Mexican term. The word means "eggs," but the reference to "balls" is so strong that you have to watch out using the word at all. Polite girls would probably order *blanquillos* from a male waiter. There are a raft of egg/balls puns and jokes.

Aside from the reproductive aspects, *huevo* means "lazy" for some reason, and is reflected in a complex of vulgar expressions like *huevón* (or *huevona*) as a synonym for *flojo* or "lazy."

There's a funny poster that says, "I failed for four reasons, *La Eva, la uva, el IVA, y el huevo.*" In other words, because of women ("Eve"), drink ("the grape"), taxes (the *Impuesto Valor Añadido,* or value added tax) and laziness. Though synonyms, *huevos* and *cojones* have different weights.

Puta

Means "prostitute," but is more extensively used. This is what a Mexican would say if he hammered his finger. *Puta madre* is so much worse, a pretty close equivalent to the modern American use of "mother f- er." *Hijo de puta* means "bastard" or "son of a bitch," but worse.

Pedo

Pedo means "fart," plain and simple. To say it politely would be *un ventoso* or *echar un ventoso*. But the word is used in several special ways, none polite. *No hay pedo* means "no big deal." And *bien pedo* (really fart) means "blind drunk."

Cabrón

Is the main "bad noun," it literally means "goatish," but is used the way Americans use "S.O.B." Can be fighting words. It is often "cleaned up" as *camión, camerón*, etc. It can be made diminutive to *cabroncito* and even *cabroncita*. *Un cabrón de siete suelas* (a seven-soled *cabrón*) is a "four door" or "24 carat" S.O.B. Also common is *cabrón de primera* (first class). A *cabronada* is the kind of thing a *cabrón* would do.

Cabronear, even in Mexico, means to be cuckolded knowingly and *cabronismo* is to prostitute one's own wife.

Pinche

Just as inexplicably, is the "bad adjective." Literally an assistant cook, it means "nasty" and is very strong. "That f-in' a-hole" would be *pinche cabrón* in Mexico.

Pues

Although the dictionary meaning is "since," *pues* (and it's colloquial variations, *pos* and *pus*) are slang expressions hard to translate but frequently used. It can be used like "Well..." at the first of a sentence (*Pues, no sé* is "Well, beats me") or as we would use "then" at the end of a phrase as in, *Ándale, pues*, (Go ahead, then) or as a general emphatic, perhaps like the New York use of "yet." An obvious question or statement can be answered, *Pos, sí.*

A Tijuana *birriería* is called *"Guadalajara, Pues,"* in the way an American deli might be called, "Brooklyn, Already."

Re-

The prefix *re-* has an augmentative effect in slang, reminiscent of the California use of "way" to mean "very." *Rebuena* is very good, *recuero* is "way stacked." *Es reloca* is "She's really nuts." Even more emphatic, less used, is *rete-. Te reteodio* is "I hate your guts." *Reteguapa* is "ultra super foxy." The ultimate lick is *requete-*, and *Estoy requeteseguro* is "I'm absolutely certain.

Mexicans use "super" as a similar prefix, as well. *Estaba super-enojada*, is "She was way irritated."

EXCLAMATIONS

¡Hijole! is a super-Mexican expression that means things like, "Oh, wow!," "Holy cow!" or "Yikes!"

Sobres is enthusiastic agreement, like "Right on!," "Really," "You said it!" or "Yeah, let's do it!"

¡Chale! on the other hand, indicates disbelief as in, "No way," "Nice try," or "Tell me another one."

¡Andale! is not only "Hurry up," but also "Get with it," "Get the lead out" and can mean either "Oh, go on with you!" or "Really!" as a reply to a statement.

¡Arriba (anything)! is like "up with" or "hooray for." One might ponder the vast spiritual superiority of crying *¡arriba!* (up) instead of "Get down!"

¡Caramba! is famous, and can be about anything from "Wow!" to "Holy cow!" *Carambas* are also curses, hassles, and badmouthing in general.

¡Carajo! is a strong, violent oath.

¡Mucha ropa! (a lot of clothes), yelled at dancers or anyone in public, is Spanish for "Take it off!"

¡Caray! is "Gosh!," "Wow!," "Holy cow!"

¡Zaz! or *¡Zas!* is like "Zap!," "Pow!," or "Oh, no!"

Nam Nam is "Yum Yum."

¡Águas! is a warning shout, like "Look out!" or "Heads up!" Ghetto slang for the same thing is *¡Trucha!* (trout) for some reason, a warning that also has tones of "Jiggers!" or "Cheese it!"

¡Arre! is "move it," but with a special tone since the word means "Giddyup" to a burro (hence, a dunce).

GUYS

Hombre is "Man," even as an ejaculation equivalent to "Oh, Man!" "Brother" to address a non-relative is not *hermano* but *'mano. Carnal* is like "Bro," but is likewise racially restricted except among extremely good friends. "Pal" would be *compadre*, more casually, *compa*, or at the slangiest, *compinche.* (Female equivalent, *comadre*, which has almost the sense of blacks using the term "sisters" or "sis."

Ese (literally, "that") is like "Hey, bud" and short for *ese vato*—"That guy" or "That cat," used as an attention getter like, "Hey, man," or "Hey, you."

Chico means "little one" or "kid," *joven* means "youngster," or "young man," appropriate for calling a waiter or polite inquiries of younger males. *Mijo* (contraction of *mi hijo*, "My son") is like "sonny" and is for younger boys or affectionately with friends.

Other terms for friends (*amigos, compañeros*) are *socio* (partner), *parna, cuate* (often *cuaderno*, which really means "notebook"), *piojo* (louse), *valedor* (or *vale* for short).

Muchacho or *chico* for young men. *Tipo* means "guy." Also very common is *chavo*. The guys are *batos* (also spelled *vatos*), *cuates, amigotes. Fulano* is "whoever" or "so and so" and *fulano, zutano, y mengano* are "Tom, Dick and Harry."

CHICKS

Properly *muchachas, chicas* or more formally *señoritas. Mija*, is used in direct address the same as *mijo* with males. *'Mana* is "sister" and very commonly used form of address. *Chulis* is like "cutie," "honey," or "dearie"—often used between women (or male homosexuals). *Nena*, appropriate for little girls, can also be used affectionately for younger women, something like "kiddo," "girly," or "baby." Can also be used indirectly, *¿Quién es la nona aquolla? Nonorra* can also be used as both indirect reference or direct address.

Mamacita is a definite come-on type of address, used like "Hey baby," to a girl passing on the street or affectionately between lovers; also *mamasota* or *mamuchis*. *Papacito* is the male equivalent, like "Daddy" used between lovers.

Indirect terms include, *tipa*, *chava*, and *morra*, all very common and acceptable terms. *Torta* is a little sexist, but means "chick." *Ruca* means "broad" in gutter talk and is not at all polite. Women as such are called *puris*, *murciélagas* (bats), *espátulas*. An ugly woman might be called *federica*, *regularsona* or *química* (*¡porque no tiene nada de física!*)

LOVERS AND OTHER DETAILS

Lovers (*amantes*) and loved ones (*queridos*) are referred to as *huesos* on the street, also as *vareda*, *pato*, and *quelite*.

Affectionate and pet terms include *muñeca*, literally doll; *preciosura*, precious; *mi tesoro*, my treasure; *ricura*, richness; and *chiquitín*, teeny tiny. *Mi amor, mi vida*, and such are used towards men and women. *Viejo* is "the old man," or husband. *Papacito* or *mijo* are endearments towards men. Wives and lovers are often referred to as *vieja* (old lady, used just as in English), or comically as *mi peor es nada*, my "better than nothing."

Girlfriends (*novias*) are referred to as *detalles* (details), *cueros* (figures), *pescados* (fish), and in the alley as *catán*.

Love affairs (*aventuras amorosas*) are *volados, aguacates, volantines,* or *movidas.*

"To flirt" is properly *coquetear,* but in Mexico is also *volarse.* While *de volada* means "suddenly," *andar de volada* also means flirting. Other terms for flirting include *dar puerta* (giving the door), *dar entrada* (giving out tickets), *pelar los dientes* (peeling the teeth), *hacer el iris* (making the iris), *mover el agua* (stirring the water), and *levantar polvo* (raising dust). "She was always flirting with the boys," could be said, *Ella levantaba polvo con los chavos,* or *Ella siempre daba entrada a los guapos.*

KIDS

There are a lot of words to use instead of *niños.* Most mean simply "small," like *chico, chiquito,* or *pequeño.* There are a lot of regional slang terms for kids, like the Mexican *chamaco,* the central American *guagua,* the Argentine *pibe.* Babies (*infantes, bebés*) are often called *bambinos* in Mexico. Other regional slang includes *buki* (as in the famous Mexican singing group "*Los Bukis*").

Educación means "upbringing," not "education" in Spanish. *Ay, que niño más bien educado,* means "What a well brought up child." A less well-behaved kid can be referred to as *travieso* (mischievous) or *escuintle* (brat), *mocoso* (literally "snot nosed"). "Spoiled" is *malcriado* and *chiquiado* means "babied" or "spoiled." You also hear the word *fresa* (strawberry) applied to brats, and also to dandies, like yuppie fashion plates. In the D.F. it originally meant straight-laced, a non-smoker of weed.

Mexicans use the word *ranchero* for "shy," so one might hear *No seas rancherita* directed to a little girl hiding behind skirts.

PARENTS AND ELDERS

Parents are *padres* in Spanish; *parientes* refers to all relatives, as does *familiares*. Mexicans refer to parents as *mis jefes* (my bosses). *Jefa* is both "mother" and "old lady" in the conjugal sense, like *vieja*—you hear people say, *Juro por mi jefecita* (I swear by my old lady). Other slang words for *madre* are *mandona, venerable, sarra, margarita*. Street slang is *angustiosa* or *angustiada* (anguished).

Primo means cousin, but is also used to mean "naive"—a hick or chump.

Suegra means "mother-in-law" (with all the same jokes and bumper stickers we have), and is frequently heard as *suegrita*.

Abuela (grandmother) is almost always used in the affectionate diminutive (*abuelita*, like "granny"). Mexican kids use *Tu abuelita* in insults much like American kids use "your mama." While one doesn't use *viejo* or *vieja* to refer to parents, *los viejos* is "the old folks."

Less kind terms for old women (*ancianas*) are *rucas, rucasianas, reliquias* (relics), *mómias* (mummies), *muñeca de antaño* (doll from yesteryear) *veteranas*. Some joking terms include the punning *Venus de mil ochocientos* (Venus from 1800), *de cuando el árbol de Noche Buena estaba en maceta* (from when the first Christmas tree was in a pot), and *cuando la Sierra Madre era señorita* (when the Sierra Madre range was unmarried).

PERSONAL CHARACTERISTICS

Many Spanish words describing people's physical and behavioral traits can be formed from root words by adding suffixes; either "...*ón*" meaning "much given to" or "...*udo*," with a sense of "characterized by." Thus words like *llorar* (to cry), *boca* (mouth), or *barriga* (belly), become *llorón*—and *lloróna*, of course—(crybaby), *bocón* (bigmouth), and *barrigón* (potbellied). Similarly, *piernas* (legs), *bigotes* (mustaches), and *pelo* (hair) can transform to *piernuda* (having shapely legs), *bigotudo* (having a mustache), and *peludo* (hairy).

Remember that in Spanish most adjectives can be used as nouns so, *Ella es muy piernuda* (She has great legs) and, *Mira aquella peluda* (Look at that hairy chick) are equally correct usages.

Other such terms include:
comelón—a glutton or piggish
cabezón—big-headed
nalgona—woman with big butt
ojón—bug-eyed
panzón—pot-bellied
pelón—shave-headed or bald
tripón—chubby or tubby
trompudo—having big lips

Latins are quite given to calling each other by such nicknames. Any group will include people called *Gordo* (Fats), *Flaco* (Slim), *Güero* (Whitey), *Chaparro* or *Chaparrito* (Shorty), and *Chato* (Snub-nose).

Other characteristics: Curly hair is called *pelo chino* for some reason, and curls are *chinos*.

Metiche means "nosy," a "buttinsky" (from *meter* to stick in).

Hocicón from *hocico* (snout), means talkative, a "jaw jacker."

Catrín means "dude," in the sense of a dandy or "high hat." The kind of person likely to be found in places of *mucho postín*, swank, plush spots.

Comodín is a sharpie or trickster.

Gorrón means a moocher or chisler, somebody who's always putting on the bite. *Pediche* means the very same thing.

Quarrelsome people are *lión* (from *lío*, a fight), *bravero, muy pavo* (very turkey) *resalsa*, or *muy nalga* (real butt).

Ruco, meaning "old" is also seen as *racalín* in the affectionate or teasing sense.

INSULTS

We mentioned *cabrón*, the kind of word men are always calling their friends in mock insult (as well as applying in genuine insult). Next most common would be *buey*, a fairly harmless word meaning "ox." But for some reason when pronounced as *guey* or *wey* (as it often is), it becomes a harsher word, not for polite company but the kind of word with which many street types end every phrase.

Pendejo is a very Mexican expletive, a poorly defined synonym for "jerk" (but originally coming from "pubic hair") and not-acceptable in polite company. *Pendejos* are known for committing *pendejadas*. All of these words are "unisex."

Synonyms for "stupid" abound and all can be converted to the desired gender: among them are the easily recognizable *crétino, idiota, imbécil* (a "unisex" word), and *estúpido*. Be careful, this is stronger in Spanish than in English and many Mexicans, particularly women, don't like being called *estúpida* even in fun. *Tonto* (fool), *menso* (female is *mensa*, much to the chagrin of members of the IQ group), and *jetón* are a few more. *Baboso* is frequently heard and comes from a root meaning "to drool" and is therefore a drooling idiot.

Noteworthy is the Spanish construction by which *por* is used to mean "because of" or "on account of." Playful constructions include:

» *Me encarcelaron por feo* (they locked me up for being ugly).
» *Fracasé por pendejo* (I failed because I was a dumb jerk).
» *Toma, por egoísta* (take this for being selfish).
» *Se busca por tonto* (wanted for stupidity).

CIGARETTES

» *Frajo* is common street slang, especially in the North. *Chilango* street slang is *menurrón*. One also hears *cartucho* or *tambillo*. Old timers still say *un chiva*. A cute local equivalent for "coffin nails" is *tacos de cáncer*.

COPS

The *policía* or *patrulla* are most often called *placas* (badges) on the streets instead of *oficial*. An underground *Chilango* term is *garfil*. There are also many terms like *azul, tamarindo, jaiba, chocolate, chocomilk* that derive from uniform color and some terms for traffic cops (like *lobo* or *feroz*) that derive from the natural Mexican hatred for the cops that hit them up for the *mordida* on the road. A cop much given to the "take" is a *mordelón*.

Being arrested (*aprehendido, arrestado, detenido*) is called by verbs like *agarrar* (grab), *torcer* (twist), *rodar* (roll), and the alley-wise *aparuscar* or *amacizar*. Or simply, *Me preguntaron, pero no me invitaron,* (They questioned me, but didn't "invite" me.) The "paddy wagon" is *júlia*.

JAIL AND PRISON

Terms for jail (*cárcel, calabozo*) or prison (*penitenciaría, prisión*) are many. Jail is often called the *tambo* or *bote* and a very common street term for prison (or *la peni*) is *la pinta*, derived from the expression *hacer pinta* (to play hookey from school).

STEALING

Street terms for *robar* include *borrar* (erase), *bajar* (lower), *pegar* (hit), *cleptomanear, pelar* (peel), *carrancear, birlar* and *trabajar con fé* (work with faith—applied to burglarizing). Thieves, properly *ladrones* or *rateros* are called *uñas* (fingernails) or *ratones* (rats) on the street.

To "squeal" is *soplar* (blow) and a "snitch" is a *rata* or *soplón*. To snitch someone off is to *poner rata* or *poner el dedo*.

Rock and Roll

A ctually, most hip Mexican rock slang is merely English. You won't need translations to speak of "punk," "heavy metal," "rap," "jazz," "blues," "country" or "rock" music. Those wishing to explore Mexican music might ask about *ranchero* or *norteño* (cowboy, country music), *cúmbia* or *música tropical* (infectious Caribbean boogie music), *baladas* (vocal music), or *bailables* (dance music).

Disco is both a record and a discotheque, a *discoteca* is a record store. "Hits" are *éxitos* or *pegaditos* hit music is *música de mucho pegue*. To play music in Spanish is *tocar*.

Along with *música rock*, there are words like *rocanrolero* (a rocker, as in the Timbiriche hit, *El Gato Rocanrolero*) and *roquear* meaning to rock, as in the expression *roqueándote toda la noche* (rocking you all night long). An expression almost sure to get a laugh is *"¡Queremos rock!"* (We want rock), a tag line of a famous television comedian.

While *cine* is "the movies," by the way, "film" is *película* and *de película* means "fabulous," like something out of a movie. *Toda la película* (the whole movie), on the other hand, means the whole nine yards, the whole song and dance, the works.

PARTY TIME

Fiestas are parties, all right, but the term more often used for partying down is *pachanga*, and "to party" is *pachanguear*. *Pachanguero* is like "party animal" and "party doll" or "party girl" would be *nena pachanguera*. Also used are *reventón* (literally, a "blowout") or *reve* for short. A *parranda* or *francachela* is a drunken spree or orgy, *tertulia* a dance party, and *frasca* or *fracas* an impromptu bash. A special Hispanic fancy is the *lunada*, a moonlight beach party.

A *borrachera* is a drunken bash, and when combined with *boda* (wedding) yields the popular pun *"bodachera"* to mean a very wet wedding. *Vacilón* means "having a ball," "feeling no pain."

EATING

Slang terms for *comer* include: *filiar*, very big in the capital, and *empacar* (to pack). Ways of saying, "Tie on the feed bag" include: *menear la quijada* (wiggle the jaw), *mover el bigote* (move the mustache). *Hambre* (hunger) can also be *ambrosia, filo* or *filomeno*. "I'm hungry," is *Tengo ambrosia* on the streets.

One hears *tortillas* called *gordas, guarnelas, guarnetas, sorias, discos* and, among the with-it, *long pleis*. Instead of *frijoles*, beans are sometimes called *balas, balines, parque, los completadores, chispolitos*, or the street word, *parraleños*.

DRINKING

While the verb "to drink" is technically *beber*, most people have learned that everyone really says *tomar*. The waiter asks, *¿Algo de tomar?*, for "Anything to drink?" and the cop asks *¿Estabas tomando?* (You been drinking?).

A drink, as in "Lets have a drink," is *un trago* from *tragar*, to swallow or gulp. Drinks are also referred to as *copas*, technically stemmed glasses. Oddly, while *jalón* (a pull) means a "snort," *empujar* (push) means to drink steadily. "Shots" or "belts" of booze are also termed *farolazos* (beams from searchlights) and *fajos* (fistfuls). *Cheve*, *chevecha*, and *chela* are slang for *cerveza* like "suds" or "brewski." In the North one hears *birria*, (actually a goat stew) for "beer," a joking "Spanishization" of American pronunciation.

A bit of drinking folklore in Mexico is that one never orders a "last" drink—the "one for the road" is *la penúltima* or, as in the old movies, *la del estribo*, literally "one for the stirrup." It's worth noting that in Mexico a *cantina* is a bar for men only. You see "Ladies' Bars" that admit both sexes.

GAMES AND SPORTS

Other than *dominos*, party and bar games generally use dice *(dados)* in games like *cubilete* (with a throwing cup) and *chingona* (with poker dice), or cards (formally *naipes*, but *gatas* in the jailhouse and streets).

A deck of cards is a *baraja* and *barajar* is to shuffle the deck. There are different games and even decks in Mexico, but you can find games of spades and poker (cribbage is unknown, alas). Poker terminology is strange, though. Aces are *ases* and kings *reyes* as expected, but queens are *cüinas* and jacks, *jotas* (the letter "j"). Four of a kind is a *poker* and full house is a *ful* (sounds like "fool"). You play for *fichas* (chips)

    You don't often find darts in Mexico, but there are *billares* (pool or billiards) and you might find *boliche* (a bowling alley).

    When watching sports you will find a proliferation of English terms, even in soccer (which most people know is called *fútbol*). You hear of the *futbolistas* making a *gol*, or being *ofsayd* (offside)—and this is more so in other sports such as *básquetbol, box, volibol* and *fútbol americano*. One hears of *jonróns* (home runs), *noqueos* (knockouts), and *cachas* (catches). You even hear the ball called *bola*, instead of *pelota*.

    There are universal terms like *equipo* (team), *empate* (a tie), *campeonato* (championship), and *temporada* (season), of course. But plays and strategies use a morass of terms that can take years to learn, so it's also usually easier to use English terms for American sports, rather than try to learn complicated Spanish translations like *medio jardinero* (middle gardener) for "center fielder" or *mariscal de campo* (field marshall) for "quarterback."

Nicknames of Origin

Is a *gringo* worse than a *chilango*?

There is a lot of slang directed at geographical origins. Americans are often politely called *americanos*, but there are those who insist that since "America" is two big continents, Americans should refer to themselves as *norteamericanos* or the ridiculously unutterable *estadounidenses*. (It should be pointed out that both Canadians and Mexicans are also North Americans and that Mexico is formally "The United States of Mexico.") This makes the familiar term *gringo* seem attractive, but it could be noted that it is a bit of a slur and might embarrass or amuse many Mexicans, like a black calling himself or allowing himself to be called a "boogie" or "sambo." A good middle ground is *gabacho*, which is applied almost exclusively to Americans, though it originally meant "Frenchman." The current slang for the French is *franchutes*.

Many Mexican regions have colorful slang terms for their natives, nicknames generally as inexplicable as "Tar heels," "Jay hawkers," and "Knickerbockers." The most common of these is *chilango*, a native of Mexico City or the surrounding Distrito Federal. *Chilangos* use the term proudly, but to others it has varying degrees of deprecation, worse even than "New Yorker" in the states. For instance, there are highway graffiti that say, *"Haz patria, mata a un chilango"*—essentially, "Be patriotic, kill a Chilango." You hear Mexico City and the D.F. called *Chilangolándia* (and the U.S. called *Gringolándia*.)

Another classic appellation is *tapatío*, a native of Guadalajara. A term of extreme pride and without the negative feel of *chilango*, *tapatío* things are very Mexican. *Ojos tapatíos* is a famous song about the distinctive European eyes of *tapatías*, and the real name for the famous "Mexican Hat Dance" is *"Jarabe Tapatío."*

People from Monterrey are called *regiomontanos* and have a reputation for being cheapskates, like our jokes stereotyping Scotsmen or Jews as "tight," but less good natured. In Mexico, by the way, "tightwad" is *codo* (elbow) and can be signified by tapping the elbow.

Other regional nicknames include:
culiche—From Culiacán, in Sinaloa
hidrocálidos—Aguascalientes
jarochos—Veracruz
jalisquillos—State of Jalisco (a slight slur)
abajeños—The lower (or *abajo*) part of Jalisco
tijuas—Tijuana
choyeros—Ciudad Constitución, B.C.
cachanilla—Baja California, specifically, Mexicali
boxito or *boshito*—the Yucatán peninsula
arascos—Michoacán
campechano—Campeche
alacrán(scorpion)—Durango
jaibo—Tampico
borinqueño—Puerto Rico
gachupin—Spain
chale—China or South East Asia
tejano—Texas

Border Slang

Border jargon (Spanglish, *inglesito*, and *cholismos*) doesn't just derive from the blending that infuriates purists on both sides; it has it's own founts of new expressions, many from the *barrios* of Tijuana and Los Angeles (or, as the *Pachucos* would say it, "*Los*"). Here's a quick glimpse at this complex web of language.

Cholos are variously L.A. street punks, Mexican American gangsters, or (according to Mexicans) any sort of low rider low-lifes that come south of the border. Though the word is ill-defined, there is a definite *Cholo* style, though it might change. *Cholos* are the cultural descendants of the *Pachucos* (or *Chucos*), who in turn followed the zoot suit Latinos of the 1950's. Much of the border lingo is their invention, although much is also coined by recent immigrants struggling with the language.

The most notable phrase in *Cholo* Spanish is "*Ese*" (that) as an address or referring to someone. Also famous are "*Ahí te huacho*" (I'll "watch" you here—I'll see you later) which is frequently stylized even more to "*Ayte guacho.*" The *Cholo caló* is characterized by phrases like *sácala* (take it out) for "spare me some dope," *tirar la vuelta* (throw the corner) for "to die," *nuestro barrio rifa sin zafos* (our neighborhood fights all the time).

Some words are merely slurred Spanish, like "*Quiubo*" from *¿Qué hubo?* to mean "What's with you?" Some are twisted down from English like a customized motorcycle; *biklas* (bikes, motorbikes) for instance, or *chopear* for "chopping" a car, *blofear* for bluffing at poker, or grabbed straight out of English like *los beíbidols*.

Others are complex puns and jokes, with syllables added on over the years until they emerge as enigmas like the famous *nariz boleada* (polished nose) to mean simply *nada*. At it's best, the border slang is free-wheeling and spontaneously creative: There is little theory behind a sign that says, *Se fixean flats* or a waitress calling for *crema de whip.*

A short glossary:

agringarse—to become "gringofied," to adopt Anglo ways
andar lurias—to be crazy, "off the rocker"
chafa—cheap, low class, "Made in Taiwan"
echarnos unas birrias—to drink (toss ourselves) some beers
gabardinos—Americans (play on *gabacho*)
jura—cops
grifo—stoned on marijuana
el mono—the movies
buti—*mucho*, a lot
loro—(parrot), friend, *amigo*
pacha—bottle, therefore "booze"
pinero—chatterbox, talkative
pielas—beers
picha—to invite
cofiro—coffee
a pincél—(artist's paintbrush) on foot, walking
tirar bronca—to raise a "beef," to bitch at someone
masticar totacha—speak (or "chew") English
no hay piri—don't worry, don't sweat it
borlo—a party
cantonear—reside (from *cantón*, house)
de bolón, pin-pon—quickly, chop-chop
tripear por burra—take a trip on a bus
clavado—(nailed) in love, having a "crush"
clavarse—read something or hear it on TV
dompear—to dump
guara—water
raite—a ride, a lift (this is spreading throughout Mexico and is hip among young people in the capital)
bobos—lazy
bonche—bunch
lonche—lunch (in Mexico, one sees *loncherías* and a *lonche* is often a submarine sandwich)

broder—brother
cachar—to catch, or a baseball catcher; this is catching on in Mexico, since *coger* (to catch) also means "to have sex" and is awkward to use
chavalo—a kid
checar—to check up, *cheques* to mean checks is now common in Mexico
donas—donuts
escuadra—a carpenter's square, therefore a "square" or "nerd"
huira—a young girl, chick
hayna—a broad, babe, honey
jale—a job or "gig"
monis—American money
lisa—(smooth) shirt
pai—pie: *pai de queso* is cheese cake
piquiniqui—picnic
panqueque—pound cake
saina—a sign, like *saina de neón*

GREETINGS AND GOODBYES

A part from the usual *¿Qué onda?*, *¿Qué transas?* is a
hip way to ask what's up or to imply "What's the
deal?" (transaction). *Bien transa*, on the other hand
means someone is a cheat. Recently you hear *¿Cómo estamos?* as a greeting. This "How are we doing?" has a friendly
ring and is good for the beginner who can't sort out which
second person form he wants to use.

Popular ways to say "See you later" are *nos vemos*
(we'll see each other) or just *luego* (later), with *al rato* (in a
little while) for short-term separations. More formally, one
usually hears *Que te vaya bien* (fare you well). *Baybay*
(pronounced "bye-bye") is considered hip in Mexico, just
as we use *"ciao,"* which is also used in Latin America and
particularly the heavily Italian Argentina, where it is spelled
"chiau."

YES, NO, PRONOUNS

Sí

Simón, is, sábanas, cilindros, sifón, cigarros, and
the *pochismo* or "Spanglish" expression, *"Claro que yes,"*
(a common expression, used in the same spirit that we
would say "Who, *moi?*"). *Claro* is, of course, the way
Spanish speakers say, "Of course," and slangsters often
express "sure," "you bet," etc. as *clarón*, or *clarinete*.

No

Nel is popular, especially on the street, and as a
sassy response like "Nope" or "Nah," you also hear *Nel
pastel*, and *Nones cantones*.

Nada **or** *no hay*

Big concepts in Mexico—*No hay, no hay* is a TV catch phrase seen on bumper stickers and decals (*calcomanías* in Spanish) and often good for a laugh. Other forms of "no got" are *nadaza, onia, nenél, nanay, ni fu, ni sopa, ni zócalo, ni marta, Negrete, Nicanor, Nicolás,* (and the Spanishized *inglesito "never in mai cochin laif").*

Ni jota and other *"ni"* expressions are often used to mean you didn't understand something. If someone says, *"¿Entiendes?"* a response of *"Ni Marta"* means "Not a word." *Ni sueños* is a comeback to keep in mind, by the way—it means "Not in your wildest dreams."

Yo

Even a simple word like "I" gets slanged. *Melón, menta, me manta, Yolanda,* and the *caló* gutter slang, *mendurria* are heard.

Tú, usted

Instead of *tú* or *ti,* slangsters often use words like *tunas, tiburcio,* and the *caló* expression *mendorasqui* for "you." It can quickly be seen here that one can improvise synonyms for *sí, no, mi* and other stock responses by playing with words that start with the same syllable.

2000 BODY PARTS

The Human Face

Just as we use words like "mug" and "map," Spanish has slang terms for the face, many stemming from the *caló* term, *fila.* They include: *filharmónica, catequismo, la feroz* (the ferocious), and *fachada* ("facade," *"Es pura facha"* means, "He's all front" or "all bluff;" *desfachatez* is "sassy").

The Human Head

Called variously *coco* (coconut), *adobe, maceta* (flower pot), *azotea* (a flat roof), *calabaza* (squash, calabash), *chiluca, choya,* and *chayote.*

Eyes are sometimes called *candorros, linternas, oclayos* or *ventanas* instead of *ojos. Caló* for "see" or "look at" replaces *ver, mirar* or *observar* with *mirujear, riflear,* or *clachar.*

The Body

La pata means "paw" or foot of an animal, but is used humorously. *Meter la pata* means "to put your foot in it" (as in your mouth). *Que mala pata* means "What a bum break," especially in South America. *Estirar la pata* (stretch out the foot), means "to kick the bucket." *Patas arriba* means "upside down," in a folksy way.

MISCELLANEOUS

alzado snooty, stuck-up
bembo a jerk, a bimbo
berrinche a tantrum
berrinchudo pouting or given to childish fits
bobo an idiot or dunce. It was popular to refer to the Mexican soap opera *Cuna de Lobos* (Cradle of Wolves) as *Cuna de Bobos.*
bruto coarse, uncouth, stupid, a redneck
bicho a bug or any tiny animal, an insignificant person, used chidingly like "twerp" or "knucklehead"
burra, veloz bicycle

bola a street brawl, a "rumble"
cabula pesado, a jerk or creep (adjective or noun)
camellar (to "camel") to walk or stroll, at the border, means to work, especially in the field
carterista a pickpocket
chabacano cheap, vulgar, common
chévere cool, hip, especially in Central America
chiflado crazy, loony, *loco*
chinche (bedbug) a pest, obnoxious person
piropo compliment, but to give lavish compliments to the opposite sex is *echar flores* (throw flowers)
conchudo (having a shell) a cynic, a "hard case"
corriente cheap, vulgar, common (said of people, or language)
cucaracha a jalopy or "beater" also *carrucha*, *carcacha*
dar color (to give color) street talk for knowing or recognizing someone, *No te doy color* is "I don't know you from Adam."
dengue prude, sissy, prissy
espantajo (scarecrow) a weirdo or "freak"
feón an ugly sucker *medio feón* (or *media feona* is "about half ugly"
güero refers to light hair or skin, thus can mean "fair," "Whitey," "Blondie." In Mexico often used as a synonym for gringo.
cantón house, is common street talk, but widely understood; also *cantera, cuartel, chantel* or *jaula* (cage); *gan* or *chachimba* are gutter slang.
changuita (little monkey) your "squeeze," your girl
fusca a pistol
grueso a punk, "greaseball," street scum, "biker"
jalonero or *jaladar* good company, a cool person to hang out with
¡lagarto! (lizard) is a cry to take away bad luck
lagartitos are pushups

lata (tin can) a hassle, bother, a pain
lépero (leper) a foul-mouthed, obscene creep, a
"gross-out artist"
ligue (from *ligar*, to tie up) means a romantic
conquest (or *conquista*, as they say)
lucha libre wrestling, especially professional style
llanta (tire) belly or "spare tire" of fat
mamón or *mamey* a jerk, a pain in the neck
mandilón (from *mandil*—apron) hen-pecked or
"apron-stringed"
muy gente ("very people") great folks, salt of the
earth, jolly good fellow
naco a nerd or hick, low class oaf
palanca (lever) pull, clout. *"Tiene palanca con el
ayuntamiento"* means "He's got pull at City Hall"
paparrucha a fib or "white lie"
encabronado —ticked off,
enojado, or phrases like *Me choca* or *Me crispa*
indicate that something tees one off.
chocante obnoxious
pichón (pigeon) a sucker, chump, or mark
gusano (worm) railroad
ranfla border slang for a custom rod or "low rider"
¡saco! said when breaking wind
li is common for *calle*, street. Also *calletana, lleca,*
and *fiusa*
tianguis swap meet, flea market
tijera (scissors) a tattle tale, a fink
tilico "wasted," starved, a walking skeleton
tocayo namesake, person (or saint) with same name
trompillo "the raspberry," farting sound with lips
quedada (one left or ignored) a wallflower
zafado crazy, *loco*
zonzo a moron, a gooner

Index

193

A

About the Author

Elizabeth Reid began learning Spanish in Junior High School at the age of twelve. She has lived near the Mexican border most of her life. She "went native" in 1985, moving to Rosarito, Baja California, to teach English to the locals for eight years.

Her love affair with the Spanish language includes a fascination for the customs of the people and an appreciation of their culture. Dr. Reid has also written a cookbook, **Bilingual Cooking,** *La Cocina Bilingüe,* with more than 100 recipes from throughout Latin America in both Spanish and English and a bilingual coloring book for children, **Moms and Dads:** *Mamis y Papis.* She also wrote **Native Speaker: Teach English and See the World,** a guide for traveling anywhere in the world and earning your way by teaching English.

In 1990 Dr. Reid established a newsletter to promote "friendly foreign language learning! ™ " She continues to divide her time between the U.S. and Mexico, and between doing translations, simultaneous interpretation and writing.

SUNBELT PUBLICATIONS

"Adventures in the Natural History and Cultural Heritage of the Californias"
A Series Edited by Lowell Lindsay

Sunbelt's Baja California Booklist

Abracadabra: Mexican Toys   Amaroma
A vibrant coffee table book that celebrates the art of handmade toys.

Backroad Baja: The Central Region   Higgenbotham
This classic off-road guide takes you to the heart of Baja.

Baja Legends: Historic Characters, Events, and Locations   Niemann
The colorful history and lore behind the peninsula's many destinations.

Baja Outpost: The Guestbook from Patchen's Cabin   Patchen
A charming book comprised of notes from visitors to a rustic Baja cabin.

Cave Paintings of Baja California, Rev. Ed.   Crosby
A full-color account of the author's journeys to world-class rock art sites.

Gateway to Alta California: The Expedition to San Diego, 1769   Crosby
The historic trek through the wilderness of northern Baja California.

Geology Terms in English and Spanish   Aurand
A pocket-sized compendium of useful terms and commonly-used phrases.

Houses of Los Cabos   Amaroma
This gorgeous book highlights the integrated architecture of Baja's Cape.

Houses by the Sea   Amaroma
A photo essay featuring stunning homes on Mexico's Pacific Coast.

Journey with A Baja Burro   Mackintosh
The author and his trusty pack burro take a 1,000-mile journey to Loreto.

Lost Cabos: The Way it Was   Jackson
The contemporary beginnings of the now-popular tourist destination.

Loreto: Baja California, First Mission and Capital   O'Neil
A history of the seaside town that was the capital of Spanish California.

Mexican Slang Plus Graffiti   Reid
The hip talk, lewd eloquence, and cool expressions of Mexican Spanish.

Mexicoland: Tales from Todos Santos   Mercer
A surprisingly eclectic group of short stories about life and love in Mexico.

Sea of Cortez Review   Redmond
A collection of contemporary Baja California stories, poems, and essays.

Spanish Lingo for the Savvy Gringo: Language, Culture, and Slang Reid
This book tells the story behind common expressions and colloquialisms.

The Other Side: Journeys in Baja California   Botello
This travel memoir spans twenty years and covers much of the peninsula.

The Baja California Travel Series   Various authors
More than a dozen titles in this hard-to-find series on Baja California history

Sunbelt books celebrate the land and its people through publications in
natural science, outdoor adventure, and regional interest.